9789042904330
I0877325

PHILOXENUS OF MABBUG
FRAGMENTS OF THE COMMENTARY ON MATTHEW AND LUKE

CORPUS
SCRIPTORUM CHRISTIANORUM ORIENTALIUM
EDITUM CONSILIO
UNIVERSITATIS CATHOLICAE AMERICAE
ET UNIVERSITATIS CATHOLICAE LOVANIENSIS

Vol. 393

SCRIPTORES SYRI
TOMUS 172

PHILOXENUS OF MABBUG

FRAGMENTS OF THE COMMENTARY ON MATTHEW AND LUKE

TRANSLATED

BY

J.W. WATT

LOUVAIN
SECRÉTARIAT DU CORPUSSCO
WAVERSEBAAN, 49
1978

ISBN 2-8017-0082-7

© 1978 by Corpus Scriptorum Christianorum Orientalium

Tous droits de reproduction, de traduction ou d'adaptation, y compris les microfilms de ce volume ou d'un autre de cette collection, réservés pour tous pays, y compris l'URSS.

Imprimerie Orientaliste, s.p.r.l., Louvain (Belgique)

D/1978/0602/8

SIGNS AND ABBREVIATIONS

BAUMSTARK, *Evangelienexegese* = A. BAUMSTARK, *Die Evangelienexegese der syrischen Monophysiten*, in *Oriens christianus*, 2 (1902), pp. 151-169; 358-389.

DE HALLEUX, *Philoxène* = A. DE HALLEUX, *Philoxène de Mabbog. Sa vie, ses écrits, sa théologie*, (Diss.) Louvain, 1963.

GRILLMEIER, *Christ* = A. GRILLMEIER, *Christ in Christian Tradition*. I : *From the Apostolic Age to Chalcedon*, London-Oxford, ^{2}1975.

GUILLAUMONT, *Kephalaia* = A. GUILLAUMONT, *Les « Kephalaia gnostica » d'Évagre le Pontique et l'histoire de l'origénisme chez les Grecs et chez les Syriens* (*Patristica Sorbonensia*, 5), Paris, 1962.

HAUSHERR, *Contemplation* = I. HAUSHERR, *Contemplation et sainteté. Une remarquable mise au point par Philoxène de Mabboug*, in *Revue d'ascétique et de mystique*, 14 (1933), pp. 171-195.

LEBON, *Monophysisme* = J. LEBON, *Le monophysisme sévérien*, (Diss.) Louvain, 1909.

LEVENE, *Genesis* = A. LEVENE, *The Early Syrian Fathers on Genesis from a Syriac MS on the Pentateuch in the Mingana Collection*, London, 1951.

Lit. = literally.

LOOFS, *Nestoriana* = F. LOOFS, *Nestoriana. Die Fragmente des Nestorius gesammelt, untersucht und herausgegeben*, Halle, 1905.

PAYNE SMITH, *Cyril* = R. PAYNE SMITH, *A Commentary upon the Gospel according to S. Luke by S. Cyril, Patriarch of Alexandria*, 2 vol., Oxford, 1859.

VÖÖBUS, *Philoxenian* = A. VÖÖBUS, *New Data for the Solution of the Problem concerning the Philoxenian Version*, in *Spiritus et veritas. Festschrift K. Kundzinš*, Eutin, 1953, pp. 169-186.

VÖÖBUS, *Studies* = A. VÖÖBUS, *Studies in the History of the Gospel Text in Syriac* (CSCO 128/Subs. 3), Louvain, 1951.

VÖÖBUS, *Versions* = A. VÖÖBUS, *Early Versions of the New Testament. Manuscript Studies* (*Papers of the Estonian Theological Society in Exile*, 6), Stockholm, 1954.

ZUNTZ, *Ancestry* = G. ZUNTZ, *The Ancestry of the Harklean New Testament* (*British Academy Supplemental Papers*, 7), London, 1945.

[ ] = translation of restored or emended text.
( ) = grammatical or explanatory supplement.

INTRODUCTION

The text of the *Commentary on the evangelists Matthew and Luke* by Philoxenus of Mabbug translated in this volume consists of fifty-seven fragments. Many of these, however, are very short, and the eleven fragments (n°s 44-46; 48-49; 51-54; 56-57) transmitted by manuscript A with the four (n°s 9-12) preserved by manuscripts B and C and fragments 27, 28, and 43 together make up over four-fifths of the extant text.

§ 1. The authenticity of the fragments

The authenticity of the fragments contained in A is scarcely open to doubt, for the manuscript was written in Mabbug while Philoxenus was bishop of the city. A major part of the extant text of this manuscript is devoted to the defence of a moderate monophysite christology *vis-à-vis* Nestorians and Eutychians, and to the exposition of a moderated "Evagrian" doctrine of *gnosis* and cosmology [1]. These themes appear regularly in the writings of Philoxenus [2].

Fragments 9-12 also deal with questions of cosmology and knowledge in the manner of Evagrius. They are treated here in a fashion entirely consistent with their exposition in fragment 49 from A [3], so we need have no hesitation in accepting the evidence of the manuscripts B and C, according to which these fragments come from Philoxenus' commentary on Matthew.

The titles in the manuscripts to fragment 27 do not specify the work of Philoxenus from which the fragment has been extracted [4], but it contains a refutation of a "dualistic" interpretation of *Mt.* 16,*16* which employs arguments similar to those found in the refutation of a "dualistic" interpretation of *Lk.* 2,*52* in fragment 49 from A [5]. It is

[1] Cf. below, pp. 10*-12*.

[2] On the theology of Philoxenus, cf. especially de Halleux, *Philoxène*, pp. 311-505; on his "Evagrianism", cf. *ibid.*, pp. 423-445.

[3] Cf. below, pp. 7,*30*-8,*29* and 56,*33*-57,*16*; 11,*11-24* and 58,*22-35*.

[4] On this question, cf. the Introduction to the volume of the text, p. 16*.

[5] Cf. below, pp. 22,*17-31* and 51,*35*-52,*21*.

therefore quite possible that the fragment does indeed belong to this work.

Fragment 28 is different in character. In it eight views on the nature of the resurrection body are described, and at the end they are all declared to be speculative. However, a *formal* parallel to this fragment can be found in fragment 56 from A [6], where the author lists various interpetations of the sentence of God upon Cain (*Gen.* 4,*15*) and ends by saying that *concerning these things everyone may think as he wishes.*

Fragment 43, which comments upon the *Nunc dimittis* and interprets *Lk.* 2,*35* as being directed *against them who at that time and now reckon him* [*sc. Jesus*] *a man and against these who run after his incomprehensibility* [7], contains nothing to cause us to doubt its authenticity, and the part of it dealing with Mary's ignorance concerning the divine nature of her son accords well with the contents of fragment 46 from A [8]. The concluding paragraph, however, reads like a liturgical addition for the feast of the Presentation [9].

The remaining fragments are all very much shorter. Some of them have points of contact with the larger fragments which, while hardly sufficient to prove their authenticity, make it reasonable to suppose that they belong to the present work. The treatment of baptism in fragments 13 and 50 recalls some of the material in fragments 52-54 (from A). The ignorance of the angels concerning the Trinity and the incarnation before the time of their revelation is a theme which appears in fragment 26 and fragment 27 (from FGH) [10]. Fragment 32 may be compared with fragment 45 (from A), both of which deal with the child Jesus in the temple (*Lk.* 2,*46*) [11]. The role of the divine life, as against human life, in vivifying the body of Christ is encountered in fragment 36 and in fragment 44 (from A) [12]. Fragment 47 recalls some words of fragment 46 (from A) [13]. On the other hand the report of fragment 16 that Christ performed miracles before his baptism

[6] Cf. below, pp. 72,*20*-73,*6*.
[7] Cf. below, p. 39,*22-23*.
[8] Cf. below, pp. 38,*26*-39,*18* and 44,*34*-45,*26*.
[9] Cf. below, pp. 40,*8*-41,*16*.
[10] Cf. below, pp. 20,*17-28* and 24,*17-20*.
[11] Cf. below, pp. 30,*10-12* and 43,*1-11*.
[12] Cf. below, pp. 32,*14-17* and 41,*26*-42,*2*.
[13] Cf. below, pp. 46,*2-3* and 45,*27-28*.

contradicts a passage from fragment 49 (from A)[14] and must therefore be considered inaccurate.

The question of the authenticity of many of the smaller fragments must therefore be left open[15], but the preceding considerations have shown that there are good grounds for accepting that at least the majority of the larger fragments, which constitute the bulk of the extant text, are authentic parts of this commentary.

§ 2. The character of the commentary

Some parts of the work consist of straightforward comment on a biblical passage, but by far the larger part of the extant text is devoted to extended doctrinal discussion, for which the biblical passage under consideration serves as a starting-point. The available evidence suggests that more doctrinal argument and exposition, through commentary on the gospel texts which Philoxenus considered especially significant, was to be found in the work than was detailed analytical commentary, although a few historical and literary comments may be found[16]. The author devotes considerable space to the presentation of his mystical and cosmological teaching[17] and to the refutation of the christological views — as he sees them — of Eutychians and especially of Nestorians[18]. There is therefore much to be said for the suggestion of de Halleux[19] that this work, the first Syriac monophysite commentary on the gospels, was designed to combat the influence of the commentaries of Diodore and Theodore, the official commentators of the Persian church and the classic expositors of the Antiochene theology. This understanding of the nature and purpose of the commentary is at any rate found in the titles to fragments 1 (manuscript P); 2 (manuscript I); 43 (manuscript E); and 47 (manuscript K).

Philoxenus seems to have written his commentary independently of

[14] Cf. below, pp. 17,*14-15* and 56,*28-29*.

[15] For further parallels between the fragments and other writings of Philoxenus, cf. de Halleux, *Philoxène*, pp. 134-150.

[16] *E.g.* fragments 5; 14; 20; 22; 24; 29; 35.

[17] Cf. below, pp. 11*-12*.

[18] Cf. below, pp. 10*-11*.

[19] *Philoxène*, p. 132.

his authoritative predecessors, Chrysostom and Cyril of Alexandria [20]. I have noticed only one passage in this work in which dependence upon Cyril's commentary on *Luke* appears possible [21]. This is noteworthy in view of the fact that "everything that the leading exponent of orthodoxy against Nestorius left behind on the interpretation of the gospels was immediately available to the Syriac theologians of the monophysite confession who were concerned with the same" [22].

The dyophysite christology with which Philoxenus takes issue in this commentary is that of the Antiochene school, and not directly that of the Chalcedonian confession. In the long anti-dyophysite section in fragment 49 [23], he divides his opponents into those who call Jesus *a righteous man, as Theodore and Nestorius understand*, and those who call him *God and a man, (a word) newly found by the heretics* [24]. This, however, is an artificial subtlety and is not likely to be a division between Nestorians and Chalcedonians, for the christology which is expressed in this "word newly found by the heretics", and which he goes on to attack, is that of the Antiochenes : *(your doctrine) confesses only the conjunction and the association of name of God and of a man ... and you follow senselessly the stupid word of Nestorius, which proclaims two natures* [25]; and *if a place has not been found... in which it is said that God and a man became one authority, power and wisdom, then there are not two as you think, and the association which you proclaim did not become* [26]. Certainly for Philoxenus all dyophysites were "Nestorians", and this frequently makes the identification of his opponents problematic, as he attributes the Antiochene theology to the Chalcedonians. But here there is no reference at all to the particular teaching of the Chalcedonians, so the "heretics" are probably "Antiochene" dyophysites, who by the time of Philoxenus were to be found mainly in the Persian church and in the eastern provinces of

[20] These two were of much greater importance to Syriac monophysite exegesis than was Ephraem. Cf. BAUMSTARK, *Evangelienexegese*, pp. 152-161.

[21] Cf. below, fragment 37, n. 4.

[22] BAUMSTARK, *Evangelienexegese*, p. 154.

[23] Cf. below, pp. 48-56.

[24] Cf. below, p. 52,*19-21*.

[25] Below, p. 52,*31-37*.

[26] Below, p. 54,*20-23*.

the Roman Empire bordering that of the Persians[27]. However, it is hard to recognise the Antiochene theology through the polemic of Philoxenus. Theodore's teaching is assimilated to Judaism[28] and Nestorius' doctrine of one *prosopon* is taken to imply a union which destroys the *idiomata* of each nature[29] — which Nestorius was most concerned to avoid[30].

It is well known that the monophysite theologians of the "moderate" camp, among whom Philoxenus was to be found, devoted much energy to the refutation of the "extreme" monophysites whose doctrine, rightly or wrongly, has been generally associated with the name of Eutyches. Fragment 51 of the present work deals with this question. At the time of Philoxenus the error attributed to the Eutychians was not the denial of the consubstantiality of Christ with men, but docetism[31]. While it is clear that rival monophysite groups did exist, it is difficult to discover the views of the "extremists" since they are known only from the writings of their opponents[32]. The charge of docetism doubtless rests on the polemical assimilation of their doctrine to gnostic and Manichean teaching, the teaching of the "moderate" monophysites themselves being subjected to the same treatment by the dyophysites. Philoxenus brings against them the usual accusations that they deny the reality of the humanity and corporality of Christ, but at one point he seems to be citing from their writings when he says: *you have delivered in writing that as the hypostasis of the Spirit appeared in the likeness of a dove, also the Son was manifested in the likeness of a man*[33]. In the present state of our knowledge about the Eutychians it is impossible to evaluate the reliability of Philoxenus' statement or to interpret the "citation" without its original context, but it deserves to be added to the list of reports on them[34].

It has long been recognised that in Philoxenus we encounter one of the outstanding figures in the history of Syriac mystical theology, who

[27] Cf. DE HALLEUX, *Philoxène*, pp. 132-133. This conclusion has been assumed above, p. 9*.

[28] Cf. below, pp. 48-51; further, DE HALLEUX, *Philoxène*, p. 358, n. 26.

[29] Cf. below, pp. 52-54.

[30] Cf. GRILLMEIER, *Christ*, pp. 461-463; 510-515.

[31] Cf. LEBON, *Monophysisme*, pp. 492-494.

[32] The information available on them has been collected and discussed in LEBON, *Monophysisme*, pp. 489-500.

[33] Cf. below, p. 64,*10-12*.

[34] Cf. above, n. 32.

was deeply influenced by, and yet not uncritical of Evagrius of Pontus[35]. Recently his position in the history of Syriac "Evagrianism" has become even more interesting as a result of the investigations into the *Kephalaia gnostica* of Evagrius by GUILLAUMONT, who has shown that the version of the *Kephalaia* commonly read by the Syrians, S_1, was not a simple translation from the Greek text, which was more accurately rendered in a later Syriac version, S_2, but a conscious revision which eliminated many of the "origenistic" elements in Evagrius' thinking. Evagrius exercised an influence on Syriac mystical theology through this version, and as a result of it among the Syrians his name did not suffer the same fate as that of Origen, as happened among the Greeks[36]. GUILLAUMONT has suggested that Philoxenus is not only the first witness to the "common version" of the *Kephalaia*, but may even have been its author[37].

This commentary of Philoxenus is a work of great importance for the study of his mystical theology[38]. Although the name of Evagrius is nowhere mentioned, his influence is evident in the extensive accounts it contains of the place of knowledge and wisdom in the purpose of God[39]. The question of Philoxenus' authorship of the "common version" of Evagrius' *Kephalaia* cannot be discussed here, but it is worth noting that the present work provides clear evidence that on many points the doctrine of Philoxenus agrees with that of the "common version" against that of the authentic version of Evagrius. Three examples may be mentioned: Philoxenus reacts against the concept of the eschatological elimination of bodies[40]; he opposes the idea of the apocatastasis[41]; and he believes that men and angels are distinct beings, not successive stages in the history of the same intellects[42].

The New Testament citations in the writings of Philoxenus are of great interest to the student of the Syriac versions of the New Testament.

[35] Cf. HAUSHERR, *Contemplation, passim.*
[36] Cf. GUILLAUMONT, *Kephalaia*, especially pp. 15-43; 102-258.
[37] Cf. *ibid.*, pp. 207-213.
[38] Cf. fragments 9-12 (below, pp. 5-16) and 49 (below, pp. 56-59).
[39] According to Philoxenus the source of his doctrine is "the Fathers" (cf. below, p. 13,*5*).
[40] Cf. GUILLAUMONT, *Kephalaia*, p. 239; below, pp. 11,*15-24*; 12,*26-27*; 58,*25-35*.
[41] Cf. GUILLAUMONT, *Kephalaia*, p. 238; below, pp. 10,*26-37*; 12,*2-12*.
[42] Cf. GUILLAUMONT, *Kephalaia*, pp. 249-252; below, pp. 57,*37*-58,*21*.

The researches of VÖÖBUS have shown that the Old Syriac version of the gospels continued in use even after the appearance of the *Peshitta*[43], and VÖÖBUS believes that "the Old Syriac Gospel text traditions had a decisive influence upon [Philoxenus]"[44], a conclusion he has reached after studying this and other works of Philoxenus[45]. In the case of this work VÖÖBUS may have overestimated the influence of the Old Syriac, for among the many texts from the gospels cited here I have been able to detect only a few Old Syriac readings[46].

The possibility of finding traces of the lost Philoxenian version makes the New Testament citations of Philoxenus particularly interesting. ZUNTZ[47] and VÖÖBUS[48] have drawn attention to readings in the biblical citations of Philoxenus, the latter in the companion work to this, the commentary on *John*, which are "something like a half-way house"[49] between the *Peshitta* and the Harklean. Many instances of the same phenomenon can be found in this commentary[50].

§3. THE DATE OF COMPOSITION

The work itself contains no references to the circumstances surrounding its composition, but the colophon of A, which gives the date of that manuscript as 510-511 A.D., provides a certain *terminus ante quem* at least for the commentary up to *Lk.* 3,*38*, which is as far as the extant text reaches. We now know that work on the Philoxenian version of the New Testament, which was issued in 507-508 A.D., had at least begun when Philoxenus was writing his commentary on *John*[51],

[43] Cf. VÖÖBUS, *Studies, passim.*

[44] *Ibid.*, p. 89.

[45] *Ibid.*, pp. 197-201.

[46] The most important are *Lk.* 2,*50* (Text, p. 45,*14*) and *Lk.* 22,*42* (Text, p. 70,*24*). The divergences from the *Peshitta* in *Lk.* 2,*32* (Text, p. 42,7), *Lk.* 3,*17* (Text, p. 17,*19*) and *Jn.* 3,*16* (Text, p. 74,*6*; p. 78,*12*) are also found in the Harklean and might therefore derive from the Philoxenian (cf. below). There are a few further more debatable instances of Old Syriac readings.

[47] Cf. ZUNTZ, *Ancestry*, pp. 40-76.

[48] Cf. VÖÖBUS, *Philoxenian, passim*; *idem.*, *Versions*, pp. 105-118.

[49] ZUNTZ, *Ancestry*, p. 41.

[50] *E.g.*: *Jn.* 7,*39* (Text, p. 52,*17*); *Rom.* 5,*10* (Text, p. 78,*5-6*); *1 Cor.* 15,*42-43* (Text, p. 32,*4-6*); *2 Cor.* 5,*16* (Text, p. 2,*15*); *Eph.* 1,*16-18* (Text, p. 10,*5-10*). Cf. also above, n. 46.

[51] Cf. DE HALLEUX, *Philoxène*, p. 122.

and it is reasonable to suppose that the present commentary was written about the same time. If both works contain readings from the new version[52], it is most natural to assume that they were written after 507 A.D., but if other considerations, outlined below, suggest an earlier date, we might leave open the possibility that the readings come from the work in progress on the new version, or were introduced into the text after the Philoxenian version was completed but before manuscript A was written.

At the time of the composition of this commentary it appears that Philoxenus' mind was occupied with the problem of the refutation of the "Antiochene" christology, the adherents of which were to be found mainly in the Persian Empire and in the neighbouring Roman provinces, and he was not concerned to refute the Chalcedonian confession[53]. After 505 A.D. the struggle with Flavian of Antioch and his "neo-Chalcedonianism" was the foremost concern of Philoxenus[54]. The commentary is thus unlikely to have been written after that date. If therefore some tension exists between this evidence and that which relates to the Philoxenian version, we shall have to be content with the statement that the work was composed sometime in the first decade of the sixth century, probably around 505 A.D.[55]

[52] Cf. above, p. 13*.
[53] Cf. above, pp. 9*-10*.
[54] Cf. DE HALLEUX, *Philoxène*, pp. 49-64.
[55] Cf. *ibid.*, pp. 132-133.

Fragment 1. Introduction [1]

Because from sin, which (is) outside of nature, the death of the body and mortality in deed received cause, quite justly mortality in deed and the death of the body is reckoned outside of nature to have entered (into it). Not that the body itself is not a mortal (being) by nature, but that in fact it was not a mortal (being). And if it is not so, how is it not found the opposite of its soul?

Fragment 2. Introduction [1]

For it is written that angels ate in the tent of Abraham [2], but it is not said that they hungered and then ate, because they were not in truth men but appeared only in human imitation. And although their appearance was a likeness and not in a true body were they revealed, we are not able to know how they appeared nor in what manner they ate and drank, because greatly and limitlessly are we insufficient to know such things which are above nature. But our Lord *ate in the sight of* his disciples even after his resurrection [3], not because he needed to eat, but in order that through food he might assure them that he had risen from the dead. And how he ate, he who rose to become the first-born to eternal life [4] and was therefore in a manner of life above flesh, should not be asked and cannot be explained, and if * someone confesses to be able to explain (it), he should not be * p. 2
believed. And like it also not how he was seen and felt [5] and showed to his disciples even his scars and *the positions of the nails* [6] and the hole of the spear [7] even after he had risen — things which it is not of miracle if before he died they had been seen in his body, because his manner of life from when he was born until he died was one (kind), and after he rose from the dead (was) another, and before he was embodied something other.

Fr. 1 [1] **Title**: Of Mar Xenaias, from the commentary of the chapters against Diodore.

Fr. 2 [1] **Title**: Of the holy Philoxenus, from the discourse which should be placed before the commentary of the chapters, as against Theodore. [2] Cf. *Gen.* 18,*1-8*. [3] *Lk.* 24,*41-43*. [4] Cf. *Col.* 1,*18*. [5] Cf. *Lk.* 24,*39*. [6] *Jn.* 20,*25*. [7] Cf. *ibid.* 20,*27*; 19,*34*.

And it is necessary to understand in him three types : before becoming man (he was) an unembodied, not composed, invisible, untouchable, impassible and immortal (one); and after he was made man (he was) he who was seen, was touched, became in needs, was tempted [8] by passions, tasted death [9] and, as it is written, *was made like us in everything except sin* [10]; and after he rose from the dead he became in that other type which Paul demonstrated and said, *Even if we knew Christ in flesh, nevertheless from now we do not know* [11]. And although he has that body which he raised up from death, nevertheless it is not a needy (one and is) an immortal, impassible and incorruptible (one) and shines always in divine glory and in an ineffable brightness and in an intense light to which there is no equal, as that type which he showed on the mountain to his disciples [12]. And Jesus is made known in these three orders which we say : first as God, and in this second as the new man, and in that third in the likeness of the angels, because men will become in the life of the angels after they rise from the dead. And the things which he promised to give to these for whom he was made man he himself first showed in his hypostasis when first he himself had been made like them, in order fittingly to show in himself these things which he would give to them. And first he was made man and was born, and he became a baby, an infant, a child and a mature man, and when he was thirty years old he was baptised by John and * p. 3 received as man anew the Holy Spirit who from * everlasting was in him as God. But he received him for us and restored him to us from whom he had been taken away because of sin, for if as man he had not received him, neither would there have been a way (by) which human nature may receive him.

FRAGMENT 3. MATT. 1,17 [1]

On that account into three parts Matthew divides the generations, because in three places the Father revealed the promise concerning his Son : to Abraham, *By your seed shall all the nations be blessed* [2]; secondly to David, *I will raise up your seed forever* [3]; (and) thirdly

[8] Cf. *Heb.* 2,*18*; 4,*15*. [9] Cf. *ibid.* 2,*9*. [10] *Ibid.* 2,*17*; 4,*15*. [11] 2*Cor.* 5,*16*.
[12] Cf. *Mt.* 17,*2*; *Mk.* 9,*3*; *Lk.* 9,29.
Fr. 3 [1] **Title** : Mar Philoxenus says. [2] *Gen.* 22,*18*; 26,*4*. [3] *Ps.* 89,*5*.

through another prophet, *David my servant shall feed them*[4]. And furthermore, for Matthew does not say the generations (were) forty-two in all, but he divided it into three parts, pointing by this to the glorious Trinity which is glorified by the new people. But furthermore, it is divisable into six parts by sevens because the Jews loved the seventh number, that is number seven.

FRAGMENT 4. MATT. 1,18[1]

For this reason it was called anointing, because the Father revealed about him through the Spirit that he is the natural Son and he is God like him, as he said, *Glorify me, Father, with that glory which I had with you*[2]. *And a voice was heard, "I have glorified and again I will glorify"*[3]. And also about the Spirit he said, *When the Holy Spirit has come*[4], *he will glorify me*[5].

FRAGMENT 5. MATT. 2,1[1] p. 4

For from many things it had been known to the Jews that the time had come to be when Christ would be born. And especially (this was so) from the weeks which Daniel wrote down[2], for at that very time they were fulfilled, and also from the prophecy of the patriarch Jacob which said : *A ruler will not fail from Judah nor a leader from between his thighs until he for whom it is laid down comes. And he is the expectation of the nations*[3]. For until Herod, who was of the Philistine race and the son of Antipater, who was taken captive when he was a child from the temple of the idols of the (said) Philistines, (until Herod) who, as I said, was raised up king over the Jews by the Romans, those who were anointed according to the law were the leaders of the Jews. And until the captivity they who were from the race of David reigned, and after they returned until John who was called Hyrcanus, who held

[4] *Ez.* 34,*23*.

Fr. 4 [1] **Introduction** : Of the holy Philoxenus. [2] *Jn.* 17,*5*. [3] *Ibid.* 12,*28*. [4] *Ibid.* 16,*13*. [5] *Ibid.*, *14*.

Frag. 5 [1] **Title** : Again of him, before these things (*follows fragments 47 ; 37-38 ; 6-8*), from the fifth chapter, concerning the time of the birth of our Lord. [2] Cf. *Dan.* 9. [3] *Gen.* 49,*10*.

simultaneously kingship and priesthood thirty-four years, the chief priests, who were also anointed ones, ruled over them. So from this John [4] Herod received (it), who reigned over the Jews thirty-seven years. And in the thirty-third year of the reign of this (man), and in the forty-third year of Augustus, Emperor of the Romans, *was born* according to the promises *in Bethlehem of Judaea* [5] our Saviour Christ [6].

Fragment 6. Matt. 2,14-15 [1]

Therefore to him who asks why Jesus *fled to Egypt* [2] we say: in
* p.5 order to cast down the idols, break the graven (images), banish * the demons, remove from them the error of polytheism by which more than anyone they were gripped, and, further, also fulfil that prophecy which foretold this about him, which he would do on his entry into Egypt [3]. And furthermore, it was fitting for him who in truth became man that he should flee as man.

Fragment 7. Matt. 2,14-15 [1]

But Joseph, however, as he had been commanded, acted first (and) led *the child and his mother and fled to Egypt* [2]. And he dwelt *there till the death of Herod* [3], more or less three years.

Fragment 8. Matt. 3,1 [1]

And twenty-five years after he returned from Egypt—for all this time is present in the interval, because when he was two years old the children were killed and he fled to Egypt [2], and after three years he returned from there, and (so) twenty-five years (it is) that

[4] Hyrcanus II seems to be mistakenly identified with John Hyrcanus. [5] *Mt.* 2,*1*; *5*; *6*. Cf. *Mic.* 5,*1*. [6] Cf. Eusebius, *Historia ecclesiastica*, I, 5-6.

Fr. 6 [1] **Title**: Again of him (*follows fragments 47; 37-38*), on (the fact) that Christ was forced to flee to Egypt. [2] *Mt.* 2,*14*. [3] Cf. *Is.* 19.

Fr. 7 [1] **Title**: Again of him, from the sixth chapter, concerning (the question) of how long Christ was in Egypt. [2] *Mt.* 2,*14* (cf. *13*). [3] *Ibid.*, *15*.

Fr. 8 [1] **Title**: From the seventh chapter. [2] Cf. *Mt.* 2,*14-16*.

he was in Nazareth — then, as Luke said, when he was thirty years old[3], he came to be baptised by John.

FRAGMENT 9. MATT. 3,1-16[1]

Therefore he who was made man is (in company) with the Father, Son; and in the virgin, embryo; and in the world, man; and under the law, * circumcised (man)[2]; and from baptism, the first-born and the new man; and on the cross, *man of sorrows and knowing sufferings*[3]; and in the grave, dead (man); and in Sheol, visitor of the souls[4]; and in Paradise, heritage-giver; and after he rose, according to the order of angels and *the first-fruits of the sleeping*[5]; and where *he was taken up*[6], king of glory; and (in company) with the Father, *God all in all*[7] and *all and in all Christ*[8]. So then the cause of the economy in flesh is this, that there might come to fulfilment *the mystery which had been hidden*[9] in the foreknowledge of God and Father[10]. And therefore was made man at the end of the times he who is begotten above the times, in order that in this dispensation the creation might be united to the creator. * p. 6

Therefore that this ineffable mystery might come to deed, the only-begotten, God the Word, became embodied. To this consummation the beginning of everything looked forward. That this new (thing) might be accomplished through the economy, *he was emptied and took the likeness of a servant*[11]. And these things, furthermore, the most wise apostle taught by (the fact) that he wrote, *I want you to know that the head of every man is Christ. But the head of woman (is) man and the head of Christ God*[12]. And *the head of man is Christ* because when he became man he was counted among men and he became the new Adam. *But the head of woman (is) man* because in the place of man to woman became also he head to the church, which indeed mystically was taken from his side[13] and was called the bride. *And the head of*

[3] Cf. *Lk.* 3,*23*.

Fr. 9 [1] **Title** B: Again of him, of the holy Mar Xenaias, from the book of the commentary of Matthew, from the [seventh?] chapter; C: Of the holy Mar Xenaias, from the book of the commentary of Matthew. [2] Cf. *Lk.* 2,*21*? *Gal.* 4,*4*? [3] *Is.* 53,*3*. [4] Cf. *1 Pet.* 3,*19*? [5] *1 Cor.* 15,*20*. [6] *Acts* 1,*2*; *9*. [7] *1 Cor.* 15,*28*. [8] *Col.* 3,*11*. [9] *Eph.* 3,*9*; *Col.* 1,*26*. [10] Cf. *1 Pet.* 1,*2*. [11] *Phil.* 2,*7*. [12] *1 Cor.* 11,*3*. [13] Cf. *Jn.* 19,*34*; *Gen.* 2,*21-23*?

Christ (is) God because the Son became lower than the Father when he became man and presented himself as inferior to him : *My Father who sent me is greater than I*[14].

And through *man*, as I think, he taught about rational natures, but through *woman* about these (natures) which do not possess reason. And through this, that he called the Son of God *Christ*, (he taught) about what has been renewed in him and gathered up as into one body, (which is,) through the mention of *man* and of *woman*, natures (both) * p. 7 rational and without reason. And (the fact) that he said * that the head of Christ is God (was) to conform with that later word of his : *When everything has been subjected to him, then he, the Son, will also be subjected to him who subjected everything to him, that God may be all in all*[15]. For irrational (natures) are subjected to rational (ones), just as woman also (is) to man. Everything with this new creation is subjected to Christ as members to the head. Also Christ the Son has been subjected to God the Father, because when he was with him and like him Lord of all and God, he was embodied and was made man, and he became head through close kinship to those to whom as creator to his creation he is by nature superior. And to them through kinship of race because he was made man he has become the head, but to the Father (he is) the obedient and subjected (one), because after everything was subjected to him — intimately and lovingly in natural closeness, like members to the head — he also was subjected to the Father as Son. And through this he subjected to him everything, because everything had in him been gathered together and united when he was subjected to the Father, and he delivered to him a kingdom in which there are no enemies nor opposition.

It is therefore necessary for those who desire to become receivers of the knowledge about these mysteries that instead of study with words, and especially of these which engender controversy, they should be steadfast in the labours of life and keep the commandments which were entrusted (to us) by our Saviour, by which they can gain wholeness of soul and a purified mind and become in impassibility, which is the manifestation of the life of the new man, (the life) which Christ lived when he was in the world. And from here they will be able to receive into themselves the knowledge of these things which (are) inward of the body, these things instruction about which we received first through

[14] *Jn.* 14,*28*. [15] *1 Cor.* 15,*28*.

the obedience of faith [16], just as also he, our Saviour, delivered to his disciples when he sent them to preach the faith about him to men: *Go out, make disciples of all peoples, and baptise them in the name of the Father and the Son and the Holy Spirit* [17].

FRAGMENT 10. MATT. 3,1-16 [1]

p. 8

Therefore the lawful way which leads to true knowledge is this: that a man first believes and is baptised. And after baptism he begins to keep the commandments, holding within himself the fear of God, the recollection of his judgement and the fear lest he grieve in anything him who is in everything holy. But the commandments are kept when a man overcomes every desire which either moves in the body or is stirred in the soul or is sown in the intelligence by demons. And when desires and the thoughts of them have been overcome, he who has overcome *puts off*, as Paul said, *the old man with his deeds and puts on the new, who is renewed in knowledge according to the image of his Creator* [2]. And he becomes the new man and a spiritual (being), in whom there is no memory of *male and of female* [3], and he stands in impassibility, which not only is not overcome by passions but also is not troubled by the memory of them. And from here, as those who know the mystery of the act say, he attains to love, which makes him who becomes in it perfect and complete and the genuine image of God. And when he has taken into himself again the likeness of his archetype — that (likeness) which was effaced by the first sin and restored back by the righteousness of Christ, the second man — as the image of God he comes upon, without veil, the knowledge of all things which have become, and hears without the ears of the flesh, sees without the eyes of the body and speaks in an unspoken word which does not receive sound from the throat nor composition of words from language.

And instead of thoughts which the impulse of the heart and the clearness of the brain set in motion, he becomes filled with wonder concerning the things which he has come to know, not only because he has been unable to bring them to sound or word or relate an

[16] *Rom.* 16,*26*. [17] *Mt.* 28,*19*.

Fr. 10 [1] **Title** B: And after a little; C: And after many things. [2] *Col.* 3,*9-10*.

[3] Cf. *Gal.* 3,*28*?

* p. 9 account about them in the language of flesh, but * also because he has sensed the knowledge that there is no way (in) which the wisdom in them may be comprehended and they be spoken compositely through embodied language, as also, rich in revelations, the apostle said, *He was caught up to three heavens*[4], and further, *He was caught up to Paradise and heard words which are not spoken, which it is not empowered to man to speak*[5]. And he called them in their place words, although here in the presence of us he said that they are not spoken, as one who had sensed that they may not be divided through construction from language and the soul does not receive knowledge about them from outside through the sound of voice and the introduction of word, but either the mind sees them when it has been purified from passions, or the Spirit shows them by revelation, as indeed he made (them) known to the holy apostles : *I have many things to say to you, but you are not able to lay hold of (them) now. But when the Spirit of truth has come, he will lead you to the whole truth*[6]. But he — the Spirit — is indeed not simply accustomed to show them to a man, but first he assists him that he may be able to *put off the old man with his deeds and may put on the new who is renewed in knowledge according to the image of his creator*[7], and then he brings him to look upon these things which are hidden and are inward of the body. Because just as the beauty of this world and the sight of everything in it is concealed from the babe who is confined within the womb, so also those things of that world and the loveliness in it and *the things which God has there prepared for those who love him*[8] (are hidden) from everyone who, like him who (is) in the womb, is still confined in the old man, for *eye has not seen and ear has not heard nor have they risen upon the heart of man the things which God has prepared for those who love him*[9].

And because, according to the import of these words, the wisdom of this mystery is not revealed by doctrine, which is received through the senses, nor by thoughts, which humanly are set in motion by the intelligence and are made to stand by blood and flesh, for this reason
* p. 10 Paul exhorted the disciples to ask in prayer that the sensation * of such things might be given to them, as also he prayed on their behalf. For he said to some, *From the day that we heard about your faith, we do*

[4] *2 Cor.* 12,*2*. [5] *Ibid., 3-4.* [6] *Jn.* 16,*12-13.* [7] *Col.* 3,*9-10.* [8] *1 Cor.* 2,*9.*
[9] *Ibid.*

not cease to pray for you and ask that you may be filled with the knowledge of the will of God in the whole wisdom and spiritual understanding[10]. And furthermore to others he wrote, *I remember you in my prayers, that the God of our Lord Jesus Christ, the Father of Glory, may give you a spirit of wisdom and of revelation in the knowledge of him, the eyes of your hearts being enlightened, that you may know what is the hope of his calling, and what is the richness of the glory of his inheritance in the saints, and what is the abundance of his power in us who believe*[11].

FRAGMENT 11. MATT. 3,1-16[1]

It was clearly made known that the angels and these other powers were not able to fulfil in everything the will of God, and for this reason it was necessary that his beloved Son, who alone was able to fulfil his will, should be revealed bodily. Where is, then, (the fact) that it was proclaimed that *the angels do his commandments and his ministers perform his will*[2]? Were they able to fulfil the whole of this? In parts only has it not been made known that they became ministers of these things of God, and to these things, furthermore, as they were revealed to them? But they were revealed as far as they were able to receive (them), and not as far as God was able to give, while the return of all to God, and the gathering up and the making new, and that everything might become in him and he in all[3] — this was kept for the Son. And its type became in the baptism, and its truth in his resurrection, but its fulfilment (will be) when all has been subjected to the Son and the Son to the Father, and God has become all in all[4].

* And because men at that time were not able to see these mysteries which commenced at the baptism—and perhaps not even the Baptist himself (could) — because they are hidden from every intelligence and are inward of every mind, but had been known only by the Father and by the Spirit, there came from them testimony in order to make known the greatness of the service which was fulfilled by the Son. And * p. 11

[10] *Col.* 1,*9*. [11] *Eph.* 1,*16-19*.

Fr. 11 [1] **Title** B : From the seventh chapter; C : Of the same, from the seventh chapter.
[2] *Ps.* 103,*20-21*. [3] Cf. *1 Cor.* 15,*28*; *Col.* 3,*11*. [4] Cf. *1 Cor.* 15,*28*.

the Father revealed that he was satisfied with it, that it alone happened according to his will. And the Spirit furthermore, by (the fact) that he rested in the likeness of a dove upon the Son, made known that *he* fulfils the service, and he preserves without alteration or change all things which became through the Son. And furthermore, he does not depart from them as (he does) from these things of the law, but here even the Trinity was revealed to show that fulfilment is with it. But also the heavens were opened to teach that the things which there became bring about a relationship to these above, and all who are born of baptism, that is of the Trinity — their return is to there if they are not unwilling to come and *to enter by the gate*[5] which was opened at that moment. But if (this is) not (the reason), why was it necessary that at that time the heavens should be opened, for was the Holy Spirit not able to go out from there without this? Because (the fact) that the heavens were opened was not needed for the voice of the Father nor for the exit of the Spirit, since it is known that a body cannot restrain spiritual nature if (the latter) wishes to pass through it — (it cannot stop) not only God, but not even one of the spiritual powers — then (the fact) that the heavens were opened made known this: that *the fence* was removed *which is set in the middle*[6] between fleshly (beings) and spiritual (beings) — (the fence) which is this composition which is seen — and corporality was being changed to spirituality, and everything which is composed to non-composition, and all things which are seen to the other order which does not fall under bodily senses.

And when everything has been made new in the Son and gathered in him as in one body — for the church, which is constituted from seen and from unseen (beings), was called the body of Christ — all
* p. 12 will become * in God the Father through the Son, except the rebellious demons and the contrary powers and error and evil which were constituted by their hands. And because these, as Paul said, he will not renew but destroy — *when he has destroyed every principality and every authority and the powers*[7]; and also *when he has put all his enemies under his feet. And the last enemy to be destroyed (is) death*[8] — therefore error and evil, which came in through Satan and became a veil in front of the mind of man, that it might not be able to see the knowledge of the truth, will come to an end. And when these things

[5] *Lk.* 13,*24*. [6] *Eph.* 2,*14*. [7] *1 Cor.* 15,*24*. [8] *Ibid.*, *25-26*.

have come to an end with their inventors, only three things will remain : the unmade Essence, the rational creation of spiritual and of corporeal[9] (beings) and the knowledge of spiritual things, which the Fathers say was placed in bodies[9]. As also the apostle said, *Three are the things which remain : faith, hope and love*[10]. And through *faith* he made known about the making new of bodies, through *hope* about the spiritual powers, but through *love* about the Essence of God, as also one of the disciples said, *God is love*[11]; but also *the greatest of them is love*[12] was put down for a demonstration that at all time God remains in his completeness.

Therefore bodies, when they have been made new through the body, will become spiritual, and with the souls and unembodied powers will become in God in an ineffable way, and he will work in them like the soul in the members, according to the meaning of *that God may become all in all*[13]. Because here bodies have been constituted to be as signs for rational (beings) that they might receive through them knowledge about God, nevertheless (it is) not (the case that), as signs are erased when the teaching in them has been received, so also the bodies in which this knowledge has been mixed will be destroyed, but they too will be made new, as I have said, through our body, in order that absolutely nothing might perish of the works of God, for *everything has been made new again in Christ, whether in heaven or on earth*[14]; but how they will be made new * and in what making they will * p. 13
appear goes beyond our mind to comprehend. And the apostle said openly, *Whether thrones or dominions or principalities or authorities or powers — all of them have been recreated in Christ*[15]. And it is clear that also these other orders of Seraphim and of Cherubim and of angels which have been made known to us through the books of the prophets, and if there is anything other which is a creature, either those which by men have been called gods or *every name which is which has been named*[16] whether in heaven or in earth[17] — all of them together in Christ have been gathered and made new, and through him have become also in God and Father, in order *that God may become in all*[18],

[9] In Philoxenus' writings *pagrā* designates the body of an organism, *gūšmā* a body in its materiality; cf. DE HALLEUX, *Philoxène*, pp. 372-373. It will be necessary for the reader to bear in mind this distinction throughout the rest of this fragment. [10] *1 Cor.* 13,*13*. [11] *1 Jn.* 4,*8*; *16*. [12] *1 Cor.* 13,*13*. [13] *Ibid.* 15,*28*. [14] *Eph.* 1,*10* (cf. *Col.* 1,*16*). [15] *Col.* 1,*16* (cf. *Eph.* 1,*10*). [16] *Eph.* 1,*21*. [17] Cf. *Eph.* 1,*10*; *Phil.* 2,*10*. [18] *1 Cor.* 15,*28*.

like the soul, and all in God, like the body, and *that God may become all in all*[18] may be fulfilled in deed. And indeed Paul draws a type like this for us by his saying that as there is no member in the body which does not have life from the soul, so also (there is) not one of the servants who does not share the divine life in that world[19], except for the demons who here have cut themselves off from the bodies of the creation and become alien to the invisible and visible (beings) — to the invisible indeed because from angels they have become demons, while to the visible because from stewards they have been made known corrupters. These, who (are) outside of this gathering up which has been made known in Christ and through him in God the Father, will be found in the place of judgement and of torment.

But these things which now have been said by us have appeared to us as in a mirror. Through the meaning of this — which we have mentioned how many times? — which the apostle said, *that God may become all in all*[20], (we learn) as also he openly taught through his other word, namely, that *now as in a mirror we see by parable, but then face to face*[21]. Because just as a mirror shows a likeness, although that likeness truly is made known in that hypostasis in which it is, even if it should happen that you break the mirror the likeness is not
* p. 14 destroyed with it but remains without damage in its essence, * so also that knowledge (about) which Paul said that here it appears *as in a mirror*, when this composition through which it has appeared to us *as in a mirror* has been removed, will gather together, all of it, to its place in Christ, and in him we as members set in the body shall see it as in *face to face*, (it) not (being true that) with sight and composition also the nature of bodies will be destroyed, as the Manicheans say.

FRAGMENT 12. MATT. 3,1-16[1]

What was set within baptism (is) therefore fire and the Spirit, in order that they might regenerate soul and body and give to each one of them that which pertains to it; to the body: the dissolution of death, the destruction of passions, renewal from corruption, peace from desires, steadiness from inclination towards sin; but to the soul: healing of the passions of sins which will not easily slip into evil, strength in

[19] Cf. *Eph.* 4,*16*; *Col.* 2,*19*. [20] *1 Cor.* 15,*28*. [21] *Ibid.* 13,*12*.

Fr. 12 [1] **Title** B: And after many things; C: After a little.

the faith, knowledge in which there is no error, purity of the mind, sight for the intellect, the destruction of opinions and of illusions, its first creation which it had before it received sin. And when it has gained such things and been purified and enlightened, it receives first, as the Fathers say, the knowledge of the truth, which is what the Maker placed in bodies when he created them, and then spiritual knowledge, which is upward of bodies and inward of composition. That (is) what at present all angels and spiritual ranks and orders in heaven breathe, take delight in, are established by and also indeed see, because on account of (the fact) that the mind of man when it has been purified sees the knowledge in bodies, (the one) which has been called the knowledge of the truth, * the minds of the powers above, which are especially subtle, see, as I have said, and also are established by that knowledge which is called spiritual. But that third knowledge which is called essential, that is of the Holy Trinity, as those say who brought us to sense such understandings — *to* it will be *made equal* all rational (beings) who here have been purified in *that world*[2]. Holy angels I say (will be made equal to it), and righteous men, after indeed they, the men, arise from death and it is dissolved and corruption destroyed. And they will become in renewal which is not composed, where they will become Christ's, (Christ) who became our head on account of the body and the members, and they will receive from him, as (do) indeed members from the natural head, an unchanging system of taste, of smell, of sight, of hearing and of touch, remaining eternally without end or corruption.

* p. 15

The soul, then, receives the knowledge of the truth when the illusions of forms and of compositions have been removed from before the mind, but the knowledge of the spirit when evil has been blotted out, while that of the Trinity when error has been elimnated, because this composition which is placed *in the middle*[3], through which also weakness is generated, prevents (it) from seeing the knowledge of the truth, as I have just said[4], while evil (prevents it from seeing) spiritual (knowledge) and error that of the Trinity. But when these have been removed, there is then nothing which will hinder the mind becoming fully in God, and *that God may become all in all*[5] will be fulfilled in deed. And because, as has been said, bodies are signs in which the

[2] Cf. *Lk*. 20,*35*. [3] Cf. *Eph*. 2,*14*. [4] Cf. above, p. 12,*13-27*? [5] *1 Cor*. 15,*28*.

knowledge of the truth is placed[6] and error and evil a veil before the mind that it might not be able to see this knowledge[7] and those which are placed in order after it, when a man has been born anew by baptism, in it and through it composition is changed by renewal from the Holy Spirit, but evil and error are completely destroyed and * p. 16 perish by the power, furthermore, * of [the same] Spirit, who[8] has been compared with fire. And Paul, encouraging us to come to this by deed and to sense this which we have become, says, *Put off the old man with all his deeds and put on the new, who is renewed in knowledge according to the image of his Creator, where there is not Gentile and Jew, circumcision and uncircumcision, barbarian, Scythian, slave, free man, but Christ all and in all*[9], for also this is as *God all in all*[10]. Therefore when the Fathers looked into the meaning of these words and similar ones, they understood and said that when these three, composition, I say, evil and ignorance have been removed, the whole of rational nature will become in Christ and through him in God and Father. (That is) according to the meaning of these (words) which we have mentioned, *Christ all and in all*[11] and *that God may become all in all*[12], while through (the fact) that the apostle said, *There is not Gentile and Jew*[13], (they understood that) he has cast out all necessity of natural and written laws and varieties of worships. And by *there is not circumcision and uncircumcision*[13] (they understood that) he has removed composition, but through *barbarian and Scythian*[13] difference of ways of life. And by *slave and free man*[13] that there is not he who subjects and he who is subjected, but by *male and of female*, for also this is set down in another place[14], (that) he has removed with composition also marriage and propagation which were necessary as long as death reigned, because to those who have become immortals it is clear that these things are not useful.

And these things will be revealed in deed after the resurrection, but in sensation and in knowledge they are received by the mind even in this life when it becomes outside the way of life of the old man and, like a babe from the womb, departs from it through the pangs of labours and of afflictions. Because just as the natural babe as long as it is within the womb cannot see this world or anything in it, so

[6] Cf. above, p. 11,*15-17*. [7] Cf. above, p. 10,*35-37*. [8] Or: which. [9] *Col.* 3,*9-11*.
[10] *1 Cor.* 15,*28*. [11] Cf. above, n. 9. [12] Cf. above, n. 10. [13] Cf. above, n. 9.
[14] *Gal.* 3,*28*.

neither is the mind which is confined in the old man able to sense the power of the world to come * or any one of these knowledges which have been related. But if a man is first born of baptism and grows in the things which befit the order of his birth and is preserved from the damages of passions and of sins, which are accustomed to ravage the birth and to tear off the members of the new man, and he continues, gaining a pure mind, according to the measure of his growth in that stature he will indeed receive the knowledges and the sensations of that world, just as also the natural man (does) with this bodily stature, because the type of that which is open is laid in this which is hidden. So that also our Lord said about this birth, *If a man is not born again he cannot see the kingdom of God*[15], and also, *If a man is not born of water and the Spirit he cannot enter the kingdom of heaven*[16]. And through *the kingdom of heaven* he made known about the knowledge of the truth and spiritual (knowledge), but through *the kingdom of God* about the knowledge of the Holy Trinity. * p. 17

And furthermore, also John the Baptist, as I think, signalled to us that we might know this doctrine by this, that he said, *Jesus will baptise with the Holy Spirit and with fire; and he holds the winnowing fork in his hand, and he will clean his threshing floor and gather the wheat into his granary and burn the straw with unquenchable fire*[17], it being clear that he called the new men who are born through the baptism of Jesus wheat, but the old man, that is the deeds of the same, about which also he said that they would be destroyed by fire, straw, for *the straw he will burn with unquenchable fire*[18]. (This is) according to the meaning of these (other words) which the apostle also wrote and said, (namely), *If a man builds on this foundation gold, silver, precious stones, pieces of wood, hay, reeds — each man's work will become known; for that Day will make (it) known, because it will be revealed with fire, and the fire will test the work of each man of what sort of manner it is. If a man's * work survives, he who builds will receive a reward; but if a [man's] work is burned up, he will suffer loss, though he himself will be delivered, but thus as through fire*[19]. To wit, the nature of man will not perish, but will be tried and made new *as through fire*; but that old (one), whose deeds have been compared with *pieces of wood* and with *hay* and with *reeds*[20], will be destroyed. Therefore body * p. 18

[15] *Jn.* 3,*3*. [16] *Ibid.*, *5*. [17] *Mt.* 3,*11-12*; *Lk.* 3,*16-17*. [18] *Ibid.* [19] *1 Cor.* 3,*12-15*.
[20] *Ibid.*

and soul, with the rest of the spiritual ranks, according to the meaning of (these) other words of Paul, will be renewed, but error and evil and the demons, who were compared with *pieces of wood* and *hay* and *reeds*[20] and *straw*[21], will be destroyed. Body and soul and the powers who have not gone astray are (the ones) who will be preserved, but evil and error and the rebellious powers (the ones) who will perish, the preserver and destroyer of these and of those being Jesus, of whom it is said that *the winnowing fork (is) in his hand and he will clean his threshing floor and gather the wheat into his granary and burn the straw with unquenchable fire*[22].

And rightly has the wheat been gathered to the granaries, because the sower sowed it[23], but the wheat received the straw *from the earth*[24]. And the husbandman has promised that what is his he will gather into his granary, because he sowed the wheat. And he will gather it, but this will come to be at the last[23], at the *second* revelation, which (is) *from heaven*[24]. But for the present in his place there has been put baptism, which by grace separates the wheat from the straw. It burns up the straw by means of the fire which is in it, but it makes new and regenerates the man who, if he is preserved, being pure, as he was born by baptism, does not need to be purified by the winnowing fork, because that from which he must be separated is not in him.

Therefore the baptism which Jesus set up is an ineffable mystery, an incomprehensible act, a deed unfathomed by the mind and the new womb which gives birth to the sons of God, in which the Trinity was revealed, the creation renewed in power, the church united to Christ, * p. 19 the rebellious powers condemned and sin * and evil destroyed. And by it mystically God (becomes) in all and all in God, and everyone who is not born of it is not reckoned a man nor counted with the living, nor is he a member in the body of the church.

FRAGMENT 13. MATT. 3,1[1]

He was baptised (of) our baptism, because he was going to give it to us, because it is a type of his death and of his resurrection. And

[21] Cf. above, n. 17. [22] *Ibid.* [23] Cf. *Mt.* 13,*24-30*; *36-43*? [24] Cf. *1 Cor.* 15,*47*.

Fr. 13 [1] **Introduction** : Philoxenus.

just as he died and rose and became for us the first-fruits from the dead [2], so he was baptised sacredly for our baptism, and immediately he gave it to us.

Fragment 14. Matt. 3,4 [1]

John was sustained by sweet roots and green herb of the earth, which in the Syriac were called *locusts and wild honey* [2]. For, forsooth, from a word which is like the equivalent of it in the Greek language, he who translated the Scripture into Aramaic thought that the gospel said that John was sustained by locusts. But the meaning of the word is thus, that he ate roots, and dwelt in the wilderness.

Fragment 15. Matt. 3,11 [1]

That is *I am not worthy to serve his body.*

Fragment 16. Matt. 4,1 p. 20

It is sought here whether Christ did signs before the fast or not. Philoxenus indeed says that he did [1].

Fragment 17. Matt. 4,3 [1]

Knowing him to be God, he joined battle with him.

Fragment 18. Matt. 4,5 [1]

For the tempter was found readily in the places which are suitable for a struggle.

[2] Cf. *1 Cor.* 15,*20*.
Fr. 14 [1] **Introduction** : Philoxenus says. [2] *Mt.* 3,*4*; *Mk.* 1,*6*.
Fr. 15 [1] **Introduction** : The holy Philoxenus.
Fr. 16 [1] Cf. Introduction, pp. 8*-9*.
Fr. 17 [1] **Introduction** *GB* : But Philoxenus said; *BS* : Of the holy Philoxenus.
Fr. 18 [1] **Introduction** : Of the holy Philoxenus.

Fragment 19. Matt. 4,11 [1]

So then that of the desire of glory is the hard (one), worse and more grievous than them all. And as Luke ordered them they are.

Fragment 20. Matt. 8,13

GB

Three (things) are sought by us concerning the centurion: one, whether he is the one in Luke [1] or not; 2, whether he was a Jew or from the Gentiles; 3, about the difference of the words of the evangelists about him. And indeed all interpreters agree that he is, and especially John and Philoxenus.

BS

This centurion is that in Luke [1]. And all interpreters testify to this, and especially Mar John and Philoxenus and Bishop Moses.

p. 21

Fragment 21. Matt. 8,24

It is right to know that God the Word when he was made flesh took that body which Adam had before he sinned. For even if the penal passions which came in upon Adam when he sinned appeared in his hypostasis, nevertheless they were not in his formation. For he was accepting them by his will and for this reason was not always tempted by them. And therefore he determined the times for his sleep, his hunger, his thirst, his fatigue, his passion and his death. So also when he slept, he slept by his will and not by necessity of nature. This understanding is of Moses Bar-Kepha. Likewise Philoxenus, Jacob of Anath and the Armenians so think.

Fragment 22. Matt. 9,2

John, Philoxenus and Moses Bar-Kepha say (in relation) to this one (that he is) different from that one [1].

Fr. 19 [1] **Introduction**: Of the holy Philoxenus.
Fr. 20 [1] Cf. *Lk.* 7,*1-10*.
Fr. 22 [1] Cf. *Jn.* 5,*2-16*.

FRAGMENT 23. MATT. 9,6[1]

For this reason he was called the Son of Man, because he became the son of the new man who preceded the transgression of the commandment.

FRAGMENT 24. MATT. 9,37[1]

The few labourers[2] : that is the doctors and prophets of the Old (Testament) who could not gather the crop into the granary of the kingdom, either because they were weak, or because the commandments of the law did not match up to this.

FRAGMENT 25. MATT. 11,11[1] p. 22

Therefore John wished to be born of this birth and become a beloved member in the spiritual body of the bride and a son and inheritor with Christ the bridegroom. But it was said to him, *The time is not now. Nevertheless, if before you I should die and rise, you will be baptised together with my disciples with the Holy Spirit and with power*[2], *but if you depart from this life before my death, you will be perfected along with those righteous (ones) who were before my revelation in flesh, those of the house of Abraham and Moses and the rest of the upright (ones) and prophets.* And that this is the meaning of this word, *Permit (it) now, that I may fulfil all righteousness*[3], other words of our Saviour make clear. For after he said to the Jews about John that he was *more than* all *the prophets*[4] and righteous (ones) and *there has not arisen among those born of women one who is greater than he*[5], he goes on and says, *A lesser in the* [*kingdom*] *of heaven is greater than he*[6], calling *a lesser* as according to the gift which John had in this life everyone who through grace is made worthy to hear and become a member in the body of the church — because there is

Fr. 23 [1] **Introduction** : Of the holy Philoxenus.
Fr. 24 [1] **Introduction** : Of the holy Philoxenus. [2] *Mt.* 9,*37*; *Lk.* 10,*2*.
Fr. 25 [1] **Title** : Of the holy Mar Xenaias of Mabbug, from the commentary of the evangelist Matthew. [2] Cf. *Acts* 1,*5*; *8*. [3] *Mt.* 3,*15*. [4] *Ibid.* 11,*9*; *Lk.* 7,*26*. [5] *Mt.* 11,*11*. [6] *Ibid.*

no one from us who would not confess to be less here than John the Baptist according to greatness, prophecy, honour and the grace of the Holy Spirit, which he received and by which he fulfilled the preaching and the baptism and these other things which he did for Christ. Nevertheless each one of the baptised, who in this life is reckoned (to be) less than John — that is by the birth from woman — in the kingdom of heaven it is made known that he is greater than he — that is by the manner of life after baptism — for a son he has become to God the Father, a brother to Christ and a member to the body of the church. And indeed greater than all these who went before him, who * p. 23 with him [were] born of women, was John the Baptist, but * he was found (to be) less than these who afterwards are born through baptism and whose honour will be revealed in the world to come, because he (was) the womb and they (are) the body, he the prophet and they the sons, he the godparent and they the inheritors.

Fragment 26. Matt. 13,16-17[1]

And what we may say (is) that it seems (to be) great, but the Scripture makes known because of it that even from the holy powers was hidden that there is a Son to God by nature and that he was going to be made flesh: *and through the church the manifold wisdom of God has been revealed to the principalities and authorities in heaven, that which* [*he had prepared*] *before the ages and* [*which*] *he effected in Jesus Christ*[2]. And if it is written in the prophet that they were declaring God holy triply[3], (that is) not contrary to the word of the apostle, because while they were declaring (him) holy they were not so understanding the mystery, the meaning of which was hidden. And neither did the demons know this mystery, and *if they had known, they would not have crucified the Lord of glory*[4] testifies (to this). And you will find many words which were spoken by the Spirit through the prophets about the Trinity and the incarnation yet which the prophets did not understand, because only the recitation of them did the Spirit deliver, and not their interpretation. As our Lord said to his disciples, *Many prophets and*

Fr. 26 [1] **Introduction** : Philoxenus of Mabbug in the commentary of Matthew, in the twenty-second chapter, taught thus. [2] *Eph.* 3,*10-11.* [3] Cf. *Is.* 6,*2.* [4] *1 Cor.* 2,*8.*

righteous (men) longed to see what you see and they did not see, and to hear what you hear and they did not hear[5], and it is clear that he who pleads to hear and to see longs because he senses. So then the prophets learned from the Spirit the words concerning the [mysteries], but the interpretation of the mysteries he did not reveal to them, because he shows to men everything which it is right and which it is proper (that men should be shown). Sometimes he delivers the word and sometimes the remembrance of [it], and at * one time the recitation * p. 24 of the word and at another time [its] sensibility — but also afterwards [its interpretation]. And it [surpasses] the measure of our thought that we should know how many are the varieties, distinctions, degrees, ascents and various sensations which there are in the divine [doctrine], even the wisdom placed in the natures which (are) in bodies. From among men there is not (to be found) he who might know, and perhaps not even (from among) the angels.

Fragment 27. Matt. 16,16-17[1]

Christ was confessed by Nathaniel: *Rabbi, you are the Son of God, you are the King of Israel*; by Andrew: he announced to *Simon his brother and said,* "*We have found the Christ*"[3]; by the Samaritan woman: *Come, see a man who told me everything that I have done. Is he perhaps the Christ?*[4]; by Martha: *I believe that you are the Christ, the Son of God, he who is coming into the world*[5]; by Simon Peter: not as these but as by revelation he said, *You are the Christ, the Son of the living God*[6]. For these confessed him Christ and Son by election and by grace. And not they only, but also all the Jews reckoned the Christ expected by them a righteous and perfect man, and greater and more glorious and more exalted than anyone in manner of life and in knowledge and in revelations and in honour, and who more than all the righteous is truly a dwelling-place of God. And indeed as he was designated Christ by these — Nathaniel and Andrew and the Samaritan woman and Martha — also the Nestorians confess

[5] *Mt.* 13,*17*.

Fr. 27 [1] **Title** F: A section of Mar Philoxenus; G: A section or explanation of Mar Philoxenus; H: Further we write a section or explanation of Mar Philoxenus of Mabbug. [2] *Jn.* 1,*49*. [3] *Ibid.*, *41*. [4] *Jn.* 4,*29*. [5] *Ibid.* 11,*27*. [6] *Mt.* 16,*16*; *Mk.* 8,*29*.

* p. 25 him today, but as * Peter confessed do we orthodox confess and believe. Therefore the followers of Nestorius will say against us, *Why do they believe about Christ an opinion which is greater than this of the Jews?* If they say that (he is) more righteous and just than all men, indeed the Jews so believe. And if they say, *Because of the purity and holiness and sanctity of his thoughts and of his members he is a dwelling-place of God*, they should also indeed think thus about the just (ones) who were with them, and thus all of them should have believed about themselves that they were temples of God, regarding which the word of God was spoken [7]. And if all the prophets and righteous (men) who kept the commandments of God are temples of God, what greater may they attribute to that man (by) which he may be named by them? And if they call him also Christ, also everyone who was thus anointed either to kingship or to priesthood was surnamed with this name. And if they call him Jesus, there also there was Jesus [8] son of Nun and Jesus [9] son of Jozadak and many others who were (there).

But the wicked Theodore says that *Thou art the Christ* pointed, as he says, to a man, namely, *Christ* is the name of a man, but the reading *Son of the living God* [10] points to God the Word [11]. And who will accept (this) from you, O stupid and senseless (one), except those who like you have gone mad? For while the Father made known about one and Simon also confessed one who is Son and who is Christ, he would deny the confesstion of Simon and the revelation of the Father and instead of one would understand Christ two. But, O deceiver, let us ask you : is that which is set down at the beginning of the word, *Thou art*, said about one or about two? If it is set down about two, * p. 26 * why does he not say, *You are*, but, *Thou art*? But if it is taken with reference to one, as it is written, of which of them is that *Thou art*? Of *Christ* or of *the Son*? If that *Thou art* goes with *Christ*, then it does not apply to *the Son*. And if it is right that *the Son* should receive it, it is not said about *Christ*.

What, therefore, (is) that Christ (of) whom Andrew said to his brother that he had been found by them [12]? What is he? Is he God or man? If he is God, why was his inquiry to his disciples necessary, and the revelation of the Father and the confession of Simon? For look, they would have known this even before the revelation. And if of a man

[7] Cf. *1 Cor.* 3,*16*; etc.? [8] *I.e.* Joshua. [9] *I.e.* Jeshua. [10] *Mt.* 16,*16*; *Mk.* 8,*29*.
[11] For Theodore's interpretation of the confession of Peter, cf. *Acta Conciliorum Oecumenicorum*, IV, 1, pp. 54-55. [12] Cf. *Jn.* 1,*41*.

Andrew said that he had found the Christ, why did Jesus give a blessing to Simon on account of this confession and say to him, *For flesh and blood has not revealed (this) to you, but my Father, he who is in heaven* [13]? For how could a blessing be given to him who confessed a man? And if he received a blessing because he confessed that man (to be) Christ, it would have been right that also to the Samaritan woman this blessing be given, and, furthermore, (that) he bring the blessing before Simon also to Nathaniel, who before anyone confessed Christ thus, and Andrew and all the Jews, because also they so confessed Christ and believed this about him, that he should be a man who was anointed and honoured by God and became Saviour and leader to their people. (It would have been right that) the blessing be given also to Martha more than Simon, for through a will glowing and filled with love, when she was asked by him if she believed that he would raise the dead, she said to him in a humble and obedient voice, *Yes Lord, I believe that you are the Christ, the Son of the living God, he who is coming into the world* [14]. And if one observes exactly, (one sees that) the confession of Martha (is) more sound and exact than that of Simon. And if * the offering of the will is honoured before God, as is written [15], * p. 27 the confession of these whom we have recounted is worthy of blessing and is honoured before God more than the confession of Simon, for they distinguished and recognised him Christ and Son of God by their will, and not by the working of a revelation as Simon understood (him).

And perhaps even Simon himself so thought about Christ as (did) Andrew and Nathaniel, because the revelation and the thinking of Simon was not from his (own) intelligence, but from a revelation of the Father. And lest they might think that as they were calling him up to this time Christ and Son of God and King of Israel thus also Simon called him, he gave him a blessing, correcting their thoughts that they might hear that the revelation of his confession which had come to be was not to him from flesh and blood. Neither Simon himself sensed the working of the revelation which he received from the Father nor did the disciples recognise (it), for the Father who gave it is unseen and also the disciples did not see (it) nor did Simon, who received (it), sense (it), and for this reason *Blessed are you* [16] and so on was necessary. But that Simon did not understand exactly what

[13] *Mt.* 16,*17*. [14] *Jn.* 11,*27*. [15] Cf. *Ps.* 40,*7-9*; *Heb.* 10,*5-10*? [16] *Mt.* 16,*17*.

had been said, all the things that were spoken and done by him after this show. First (there is the fact) that he was rash from zeal and *restrained* his master *and said to him*, "*Far be it from you, my Lord, that this should happen to you*" [17], when he was speaking because of passion. But Jesus, rejecting his evil, said to him, *Go you behind me, Satan!* [18] to show that Satan had sown this word in his heart. And just as Satan sowed this doubt in the soul of Simon and effected that he say a word which is in opposition to the whole economy and a damage to the whole world, and *he did not know what he was saying*, so he received a revelation from the Father and proclaimed Christ God * p. 28 and the natural Son, *while not knowing* * *what he was saying* [until Jesus revealed to him that he had received (it) from the Father. And further he said, *not knowing what he was saying* [19],] "*It is well that we are here, and let us make three booths*" [20]. And as the words which he spoke (were) amazing and awful and mysterious, he did not understand the meaning of his words. Therefore it is written about him that *he did not know what he was saying* [21]. For not even the demons knew this mystery at that time, and even from the angels this was hidden, that they should know that there is a Son to God by nature and he was going to fulfil in his hypostasis the mystery of the new economy of men. For men know nothing of spiritual things and the knowledge of the world to come is entirely hidden from us, as the knowledge of this world is hidden from (one) a day old. So let us not marvel that a revelation came to Simon and he did not sense its meaning, while the truth was made manifest through the revelation and Christ was made known to be not a man according to the opinion of the Jews, but the Son of God as the Father revealed him.

Therefore he who confesses Christ as the Father taught about him, he indeed is justly called by his name, that is Christian. But if he understands Christ otherwise, according to the opinion of the Nestorians or Arians or as the Jews or heathen think about Christ, he does not recognise the Christ whom the Father revealed through Simon, but the false Christ who is to come [22] and of whom (this) word of Jesus is rightly said : *I have come in my Father's name and you do not receive me. And if another comes in his own name, him you will receive* [23]. And just as the expectation of the Jews to this very day

[17] *Ibid., 22.* [18] *Ibid., 23.* [19] *Mk. 9,6*; *Lk. 9,33.* [20] *Mt.* 17,*4*; *Mk. 9,5*; *Lk. 9,33.* [21] Cf. above, n. 19. [22] Cf. *1 Jn. 2,18*; 4,*3*. [23] *Jn.* 5,*43*.

looks to the false Christ, so also * it is clear that the heretics who do * p. 29 not confess Christ as Simon confessed him by the revelation of the hidden Father await the false Christ. And (this is true) although they contend against it so much. Therefore it is manifest that everyone who forsakes the confession of one Christ who is true God holds to another Christ, who is the Antichrist or one of these (about) whom our Lord said, *False Christs and prophets of treachery will come*[24], and *Many will come in my name and say, "I am the Christ"*[25], which although they are many, nevertheless all of whose working (is) with one countenance. For just as they took the name *Christs* from this true Christ and placed (it) upon themselves, so also in deeds and in rites of defilement they imitate that false Christ, that the name might be from one, the deed from the other. As also the demons named themselves from the true God and taught men to reckon them gods[26], and while the name was taken from God. their own is the evil of the works and the abomination of the deeds. Therefore it is manifest that he who denies this name believes in one of these. And *the coming of that one*, according to the word of Paul, *is the working of Satan*[27]. So the god of the heretics is Satan, even if the word (God) (is) dear to them.

FRAGMENT 28. MATT. 22, 29-32[1]

Some indeed say that only thickness will be taken from the body, while the entire form of its members and of its senses will remain as it is.

* But others say that not even the thickness of the body will be taken * p. 30 away from it, but being in the type of its composition now — flesh, nerves, hair and nails with the rest of the viscera — (there) will only be given to it swiftness, movement and acuteness.

But there are others who say, and add to this opinion, that while so remaining in its thickness, (there) will come to it power which it may use as it wills, so that it may enter even by closed doors if it wishes, and also may float in air and may walk upon the waters. And they

[24] *Mt.* 24,*24*; *Mk.* 13,*22*. [25] *Mt.* 24,*5*; *Mk.* 13,*6*; *Lk.* 21,*8*. [26] Cf. *Ez.* 28,*2*; *2 Thess.* 2,*4*; *1 Cor.* 8,*4-6*; *Gal.* 4,*8*. [27] Cf. *2 Thess.* 2,*9*.

Fr. 28 [1] **Introduction** : Chapter fourteen, which shows what those of former times thought about the resurrection of bodies and about the manner of their resurrection. Of the holy Philoxenus, from the commentary of Matthew.

infer and construct (these) opinions from (the fact) that our Lord *walked upon the waters* and made also Simon to walk like him[2], and also (from the fact that) after his resurrection he entered *while the doors were shut*[3] and after he entered showed *the positions of the nails*[4] and of the spear[5], as in a thick body.

But there are others who say that all men will rise in one measure, that is compositely and bodily, and all of them will become like that stature of Christ in which he came to baptism. And whether these who are brought are found under [this stature] or over it, they will all become like the stature of Christ. And they understand this, as they wish (it), from (the fact) that Paul said, *Until we shall all become one in the faith and in the knowledge of the Son of God, and one man complete in the measure of the stature of the fullness of Christ*[6]. And they have likened that thickness which (is) their opinion to the spiritual word of Paul, and according to this composition in which men rise, as they say, they will see with the eyes, hear with the ears, smell with the nose, taste with the palate and touch [with] the corporeality of the body, who from this opinion which is being shown will also continue in this thickness of the elements.

But others do not accept these things which have been said, but say: (it is) so that this body which fell, it will rise, because resurrection
* p. 31 is promised to it in the Holy Scriptures. But it will rise through * a spiritual change and become a different likeness. (They say) that it will not be like the angels nor remain according to the type of its first composition, but that the same body, truly that which fell, will rise. Something other, which differs from that first (one), will appear, according to the example of the grain of wheat which Paul used when telling about the resurrection[7]. Namely, that just as the same grain of wheat when it has decayed in the earth becomes by an amazing change something other which is not like its beginning nor its end — and while the stalk [and] the nodes and the sight of the blade and the calyxes and the beards are not like the nature of that grain of wheat which was sown, while it is that which [appears] in all of these by an amazing change — so also, namely, the bodies of men which are sown in graves like wheat in furrows will come to an amazing and

[2] Cf. *Mt.* 14,*25-31*. [3] *Jn.* 20,*26*. [4] *Ibid.*, *25*. [5] Cf. *ibid.*; *Jn.* 19,*34*. [6] *Eph.* 4,*13*.
[7] Cf. *1 Cor.* 15,*37*.

exalting change and become a comely and adorned likeness which (is) much more exalted and glorious than their first construction.

But others say: compositely and with the appearance of stature all men will rise, but the righteous [must] put on the glory and brilliance which we have said that Adam had before the transgression of the commandment, which was spread upon Moses [8] (and) in which *Moses and Elijah appeared* when they came to Jesus [9], as also about our Lord it is written that *his face shone as the sun and his garments became white as snow* [10].

But there are others who outside of all these (things) think otherwise and truly and correctly confess the resurrection of bodies, but say that its former likeness will not appear in it at all, just as also in its construction, in its composition and in its corporeality the likeness of the seed from which it came into being does not appear. But just as from a natural seed a body comes into being with all the members, nerves, bones, hair and nails and (the senses of) hearing, smell, sight and taste, all of these, which (are) from the seed, which very same seed they are not like — that is it becomes all of them by that change * with the appearance of which there is no likeness or image, or the * p. 32
composition of one of the senses or members — so also the human body will come through the resurrection to spiritual renewal and in everything become in the likeness of the angels. As Paul said, *It is sown in corruption, it rises without corruption, it is sown in dishonour, it rises in glory, it is sown in weakness, it rises in power, it is sown an animal body and rises a spiritual body* [11]. As they were saying that it will become a spiritual (being) not only in its way of life but in nature, as also the holy angels in their ways of life and in their nature are [spiritual (beings)], and because it will not rise a composite and embodied (being), they say that it will see with its entirety, hear with its entirety, taste with its entirety and smell with its entirety, not dividing to it the office of the senses according to what is in this composition, because, namely, the angels are thus, that they do not see with (one) part and hear with another and speak with another, for these (parts), where they are, thus manifest composition. And (so), namely, it is not to be acknowledged that part of it will be body and part of it soul, that is (there) will not become a two-fold (being formed) of body and soul.

[8] Cf. *Ex.* 34,*29-35*; *2 Cor.* 3,*7-18*. [9] *Mt.* 17,*3*; *Mk.* 9,*4*; *Lk.* 9,*30-31*. [10] *Mt.* 17,*2* (cf. *Mk.* 9,*3*). [11] *1 Cor.* 15,*42-44*.

And the soul will not receive doctrine and knowledge through its (—the body's—) senses as is (the case) with it here, but the body will in everything be changed rationally and become as the nature of the soul, while indeed the soul itself will receive another renewal in everything. Not only will it obtain a change from evil to good and from error to knowledge, but also its very nature will receive renewal that it might become something other which will surpass what it is (now). And even if we do not know to say how, through (the fact) that it will obtain strength and power as the angels (have), and swiftness and brilliance, (it will become) in everything like them. And they who say this are sustained upon this belief by the meaning of that word of our Lord to the Pharisees and Sadducees, that *they who have deserved that age and the resurrection from the dead will not take wives nor become wives to husbands*, neither eat nor drink, *but will be* * p. 33 *as the angels * of God because they will have become sons of the resurrection*[12]. And from this word and from others like it which were spoken by Christ, they say that not only in ways of life will the body become a spiritual (being) in the type of the angels, while no difference at all will appear between [it] and the soul nor between both of them and the order of angels, but body and soul will come into one nature and a spiritual hypostasis and in everything (be) without change or alteration. But this man will be like the holy angels.

But, furthermore, others agree with and accept and believe all these things which have been said in this part, that will become soul and body, the two of them, one man and one spiritual nature and in everything be as the holy angels, in spirituality and in ways of life, (but) say that in this spirituality differentiation will be found and in the spiritual construction order will separate from order and class from class. As angels differ from cherubim, cherubim from seraphim, seraphim from thrones, thrones from dominions, dominions from authorities, authorities from principalities and principalities from powers, for while all of these are one spiritual nature and one glorious and exalted creation there are separations and differences in this spirituality, even if we do not know to liken or speak them, so also (as regards) perfected and righteous men when in the renewal they will be made like this spirituality, they say that their order and their office will differ from that of the angels, although they also will be

[12] *Lk.* 20,*35-36* (cf. *Mt.* 22,*30*).

in everything like them spiritual (beings) and become with those (ones) spiritual and holy powers in that world of spirit. A two-fold world, lower and upper, corporeal and spiritual, will not come into being, but everything will be gathered up and made new and a world of spirit, neither composite nor embodied, will come into being, in which all holy and spiritual powers will dwell, delighting constantly and without satiation in the revealed and unsatiating light * of the Holy Trinity. * p. 34 And these things are said by them about the righteous and perfected, but about the evil and about the wicked they say that in everything they will be made like the demons, while their bodies and their souls, even theirs, will become one spiritual nature. (The fact) that their spirituality will become like the demons, and not like the angels, (is) in order that by this they may receive that punishment which is decreed for them without end, as they are to be condemned in that nature which is spiritual.

Therefore we tell all these as we have found (it) and as others have thought with its many variations. But the truth, the [accurate (thing)] of that part which is the lasting and steadfast (one) of these which have been told, is revealed only to the knowledge of God. For truly the entire search into spiritual (things) is told by everyone in supposition. If one should seek something more outside of these things which are clearly and openly set down in the Scriptures, one cannot understand.

Fragment 29. Matt. 26,23[1]

Even if all the disciples stretched out with him their hands into the dish, nevertheless when our Lord stretched out his hand, they withdrew their hands. But Judas (did) not (do) so, but with him insolently stretched out his hand equally. And this is (the meaning of) *he who dips his hand*[2]. And while from this the disciples did not recognise the betrayer, *he dipped the bread and gave to him*[3], and immediately they knew him.

Fr. 29 [1] **Introduction** : Of the holy Philoxenus. [2] *Mt.* 26,*23*. [3] *Jn.* 13,*26*.

Fragment 30. Matt. 26,26-29[1]

Our Lord ate from his body and drank from his blood.

p. 35

Fragment 31. Matt. 26,29[1]

GB

Until Judas went out, our Lord did not give his body.

BS

He did not make him a partaker in the mysteries, because Satan at that time was already entering into him.

Fragment 32. Matt. 26,36-44[1]

He brought questions to the scribes and to the doctors[2], and because of them he gave to us the interpretation of the spiritual mysteries. He sweated when the compulsion of the fear of death ruled over him[3], and he wiped from us that *in the sweat of your face you shall eat bread*[4].

Fragment 33. Matt. 27,45-53[1]

Therefore the first man, as the account of the divine Scriptures shows us, was created by God at the first hour of the day. And at his very creation he had been named the image of God and the likeness, but not only was he (so) named, but also he (so) became. And for a demonstration of his honour and of the authority which had been given to him, *he called the names to all the cattle and*

Fr. 30 [1] **Title** : Philoxenus said.

Fr. 31 [1] **Introduction** *GB* : Philoxenus denied (it), who said in the commentary of Matthew; *BS* : Philoxenus of Mabbug in the commentary of Matthew says. Cf. *Horreum*, p. 63.

Fr. 32 [1] **Title** : Of Mar Xenaias, from the second book of the commentary of Matthew, from the twenty-ninth chapter. [2] Cf. *Lk.* 2,*46*. [3] Cf. *ibid.* 22,*44*. [4] *Gen.* 3,*19*.

Fr. 33 [1] **Title** : Of the holy Philoxenus, from the commentary of Matthew, from the twenty-ninth chapter.

animals and birds[2], when in the economy and by the direction of God they passed before him. And he called each one of the races by its name, and these things happened until the third hour. But at it, at this time of the third hour, * *the Lord God caused a stillness to fall upon Adam, and he slept, and he took a rib from his side and constructed a woman*[3]. And at that time of the third hour they were both placed in the garden and received the commandment from God. At the third hour, at which Adam and Eve entered the garden and received the commandment, according to the word of the evangelist Mark, our Lord was crucified: *It was the third hour when they crucified him*[4]. And at the time of the sixth hour Adam departed from the commandment[5] which had been laid upon him and stretched out his hand and plucked and ate of the fruit[6]. That he transgressed the commandment and knew his own nakedness[7] — on this account all creatures [were *saddened and grieved*][8]. Therefore at that time when Adam transgressed the commandment and knew that he had been stripped naked, all creatures [mourned] with him and on account of him. And also at this time *the sun was darkened* at the crucifixion[9]. * p. 36

FRAGMENT 34. MATT. 27,45-53[1]

Adam, when he transgressed the commandment and ate of the fruit, immediately became a mortal. He attempted and sought that, if there had been a way, he might not die. And he reckoned to draw near (and) eat from the tree of life, which had been given to him with the promise of the observance of the commandment, and annul from himself the sentence of death which had come in upon him. And this he desired to do, presumptuously and not in its season. But when God saw what further his presumption was planned to effect, he swiftly hastened and expelled him from the garden, saying, *Lest he stretch out his hand and take also from the tree of life, and eat, and live forever*[2].

[2] *Gen.* 2,*20*. [3] *Ibid.*, *21-22*. [4] *Mk.* 15,*25*. [5] Cf. LEVENE, *Genesis*, pp. 78; 154-155. [6] Cf. *Gen.* 3,*22*. [7] Cf. *ibid.*, *7*. [8] Cf. *Mk.* 14,*33*? [9] *Lk.* 23,*45*.

Fr. 34 [1] **Title**: And after other things. [2] *Gen.* 3,*22*.

p. 37

Fragment 35. Matt. 27,56 [1]

Joseph and Cleopas (were) brothers, and Mary the mother of Christ and Mary (the wife) of Cleopas sisters, and these two brothers took (as wives) these two sisters.

Fragment 36. Luke 1,35 [1]

God the Word and the flesh from Mary at once rushed towards union, and after *the Word became flesh* [2], as John said, and remained forty days in members and in forms, it received a rational soul according to the order of men — that after the body is made complete in members and in forms after forty days, it received a soul — as is clear in this, from that *the Word became flesh*, as in that *he became flesh* he says that he was united to flesh. And if someone says that that flesh was dead in these forty days, he answers that it was living, because it lived with the life of the divinity of the Word. And also on the cross, when the soul was separated from the body, the body too lived with the life of his divinity, because (his divinity) was not separated from either one of them.

Fragment 37. Luke 2,7 [1]

But (as to) that (question) of why Jesus Christ was born in a cave and laid in a manger [2], with (the fact) that they make known his
* p. 38 lowliness * and his emptying, they also show other things which are on the level of spiritual sight. For because the race of men by the first transgression of the commandment annulled its honour and was made like cattle, as the word of prophecy makes known [3], to where this

Fr. 35 [1] **Introduction**: Cyril and Severus and Philoxenus say that Mary the mother of God and *Mary (the wife) of Cleopas* were sisters. And he calls her *the sister of his mother* (*Jn.* 19,*25*). Of the holy Philoxenus. Cf. *Horreum*, p. 71; *Versio Harclensis*, marginal note on *Jn.* 19,*25*.

Fr. 36 [1] **Introduction**: Philoxenus says. Cf. *Candélabre*, p. 42. [2] *Jn.* 1,*14*.

Fr. 37 [1] **Title**: Again of him, before these (*follows fragment 47*), from the thirty-second chapter, commentary on *Our Lord was born in a cave and laid in a manger*. [2] Cf. *Lk.* 2,7. [3] Cf. *Is.* 1,*3*?

race which had been made like animals turned, there Jesus was laid before them in the place of their food. Because the manger is the place which receives the food of animals — as also the womb is the position of the becoming of men, the uterus is the gate through which they pass out into the world, swaddling clothes the garment of their infancy, arms and knees the carrying and the up-bringing of their childhood, and also breasts the sources of their nourishment, and so on, and as Jesus was involved in all these things of the growth of men — so also he was laid in the manger of the animals, as indeed towards this turned these for whose salvation he came [4].

Fragment 38. Luke 2,7 [1]

Therefore I understand that the cave had been fashioned a type of the tomb of Christ, because it is written also about it that it was a cave [2], the manger a figure of the cross and of the altar, and the swaddling clothes in which he was wrapped when he was laid in the manger [3] the mark of the old man who had been *nailed to the cross* as Paul said [4], in that *he bore all our sins and took them up in his body to the cross* [5].

Fragment 39. Luke 2,21 [1]

But the blasphemers say, *If * something had been cut off from his body* * p. 39 *in circumcision, they would have shown to us what became from that part of the flesh which had been torn out, by which, if it had been thrown into the earth and corrupted, would be made false that (word) of the prophet (in) which he said, "Thou wilt not give thy Holy (One) to see corruption"* [2]. But if this is not fit to be considered, that according to what they say Jesus was not circumcised stands, and they

[4] Cf. Payne Smith, *Cyril*, p. 11.

Fr. 38 [1] **Title**: And further. [2] Cf. *Mt.* 27,*60*; *Mk.* 15,*46*; *Lk.* 23,*53*. [3] Cf. *Lk.* 2,7. [4] Cf. *Col.* 2,*14*. [5] *1 Pet.* 2,*24*.

Fr. 39 [1] **Title**: Of the holy Mar Xenaias, bishop of Mabbug, from the discourse on *Her days when she should give birth were fulfilled, and she gave birth to her first-born son* (*Lk.* 2,6-7), speaking about the circumcision of our Lord (*Lk.* 2,*21*). [2] *Ps.* 16,*10*; *Acts* 2,*27*; 13,*35*.

utter things which are appropriate to the Manicheans, as they are reckoned by the church.

Fragment 40. Luke 2,21[1]

Therefore we do not say that *his body saw corruption*[2], nor do we presume to ask what became from the cutting of his circumcision.

Fragment 41. Luke 2,21[1]

For if they remain in the presumption, being propped up without understanding by the exterior of that word of Scripture which says that *his body did not see corruption*[2], they should learn from where it is written that it is said not about the circumcision, but about the resurrection.

Fragment 42. Luke 2,21[1]

And if thus a mystery of his economy is this, believe that even the cutting of the circumcision of Christ was united to his hypostasis in the resurrection, and corruption did not have dominion over it[2] as the living and life-giving body of God! And do not impiously seek out where that part was until the time of the resurrection!

p. 40 Fragment 43. Luke 2,22-39[1]

Therefore all the offerings of animals *which were offered according*

Fr. 40 [1] **Title**: And further. [2] Cf. *Acts* 2,*31*.
Fr. 41 [1] **Title**: And further. [2] *Acts* 2,*31*.
Fr. 42 [1] **Title**: And further, at the end of the discourse. [2] Cf. *Rom.* 6,*9*.
Fr. 43 [1] **Title** D: The commentary of the gospel of Luke, which was done by Philoxenus of Mabbug. It is fitting that it should be read at the feast of the ὑπάντησις. And after a few things; E: From the commentary of chapters of the gospel of Luke, against which (chapters) the Nestorians stumble, which was done by Philoxenus, bishop of Mabbug. It is fitting that it should be read at the feast of the ὑπάντησις, that is of the Entry. And after a few things.

to the law[2] (were) a figure and their offering was showing the great sacrifice of Christ[3]. And for this reason was offered *the bull calf*[4] *in which there is no blemish*[5], because Christ too was named *the fatted bull*[6]. And also the ram, the lamb and the sheep were offered, for Jesus too was called by these names : *As a lamb he was led to the slaughter and as a sheep before the shearer he was silent*[7]; and further, *Behold the lamb of God which takes away the sin of the world*[8]. But the kid of the goats was offered for sins[9] for it was a type of the sin which Christ slew on his cross. But furthermore, were offered the turtle-dove and the young dove[10], but the rather for purification, for Jesus was called by the name of the turtle-dove and received the likeness of a dove : *The voice of the turtle-dove was heard in our land*[11]; and *I saw the Spirit of God descending like a dove, and it came upon him*[12]. And before the offering of his hypostasis the names by which he was to be called were offered for sins and purifications. And with the type his names absolved, but with the truth his real hypostasis. Therefore his hypostasis touches his name with the turtle-dove because his hypostasis was to be offered for sins, but (in the case of) the young dove because the offering itself was sanctified by the Spirit, as also priests today sanctify by the Spirit the sacrifice which is offered.

But to these things the evangelist adds the things which happened in the temple when Jesus entered and relates the story of Simeon and of Anna. And about * Simeon he said that *he was a just and righteous (one)* * p. 41
and was in expectation[13]; and he prayed for others' good things, because it — compassion towards men and that it may ask of God good things for everyone — accompanies righteousness. And on account of his virtues and the good will which he possessed for his compatriots, that is for the Israel of God, there was given to him (as) reward the Holy Spirit, who revealed beforehand to him *that he would not* taste *death until he see* God being revealed upon the earth and being with men, (God) whom the evangelist called in this place *the Christ of the Lord*[14]. And also Simon confessed him by revelation to be *the Christ of the Lord*[15], and furthermore all the apostles proclaimed to him, *We have believed and have come to know that you are the*

[2] *Heb.* 10,*8*. [3] Cf. *ibid.* 8-10. [4] Cf. *Lev.* 4,*3*; *14*. [5] Cf. *Num.* 19,*2*; *Lev.* 4,*3*. [6] Cf. *Lk.* 15,*23*; *27*; *30*. [7] *Is.* 53,*7*. [8] *Jn.* 1,*29*. [9] Cf. *Lev.* 4,*23*; etc. [10] Cf. *Gen.* 15,*9*; *Lev.* 1,*4*; etc. [11] *Cant.* 2,*12*. [12] *Jn.* 1,*32*. [13] *Lk.* 2,*25*. [14] *Ibid.*, *26*. [15] Cf. *Mt.* 16,*16*; *Mk.* 8,*29*; *Lk.* 9,*20*.

Christ, the Son of the living God[16]. Therefore to this just man in the hour that Jesus entered the temple was revealed by the Holy Spirit, *Your expectation has arrived, the Saviour of Israel has been revealed and the good of the world which you desired to see has come.* And diligently he arose and hastened to the temple of God and went ahead and stood in the temple before him. Because he was a priest, and no doubt the time of service was his, with authority *he took* Jesus *in his arms*[17], since the priests were accustomed to receive the firstborn, who were offered to God. But he not only as a priest received Jesus, but also as a just and righteous (man) and a prophet. For this reason indeed he had been bound by the Holy Spirit to this life, that he might preach about the Saviour and then be counted with the saved, that from every side the greatness of Christ might be seen and he might be revealed to be God, not only from the wonders which happened in his conception, in his birth and in his growth, but also from the heralds who announced about him — (heralds) as Zechariah was, and Elizabeth and John, and before them the angel who announced about his conception, and as was Anna the widow who (was) the
* p. 42 daughter of Phanuel, * (Anna) who was filled, along with chastity and holiness, also with the Holy Spirit.

Therefore, when Simeon *took* Jesus *in his arms he blessed God and said*, "*Now release thou thy servant according to thy word in peace; for behold, mine eyes have seen thy favour which thou hast prepared in the face of all peoples, light for revelation of the nations and glory of thy people Israel*"[18]. Therefore be it to God the Father or to Jesus his Son, whom Simeon was bearing, (that) we understand these words to be spoken, both may fit the truth. But to the heretics there is no doubt about (the fact) that (they are spoken only) to God the Father. For they say that Simeon was praying to him and petitioning him, because about these words they contend they do not fit him whom he was bearing, the babe in his arms. Let us ask them why they are not appropriate to Jesus. Surely not because he said, *Now release thy servant, my Lord*? Yet look, the apostle called himself his servant at the beginning of his book : *Paul, servant of Jesus Christ*[19]. And if (that is) not (the reason), does (the fact) that he (—Simeon—) was seeking that he might release him from life not accord with him (—Jesus)? Yet how could he who by his command authoritatively restored and

[16] *Jn.* 6,69. [17] *Lk.* 2,28. [18] *Ibid.*, 28-30. [19] *Rom.* 1,*1*.

restores men from death to life not have had the authority to release from life? But if not (that), is *Behold, mine eyes have seen thy favour* not of him? Yet look, Zechariah said about him, *He has done favour with our Fathers and has remembered his holy covenants*[20]. And if not (that), do they say that (the fact) that he called him *light* which was given to *the nations for revelation* is not right for him? Yet how did prophecy fore-proclaim him light[21]? But if they should say that he is not the *Lord*, the *God* of Israel, (behold) the word of Zechariah which confutes their opinions, for he prophesied about his son, *You, child, will be called the prophet of God. You will go before the face of the Lord to prepare his way, that he might give knowledge of salvation to his people in the forgiveness of their sins*[22]. And the angel said, * *She* * p. 43 *will give birth to a son and you shall call his name Jesus. For he will save his people from their sins*[23]. But if they are doubtful about (the fact) that he blessed God whom he was bearing in his arms as it does not fit that babe [that he should be believed God, an angel called that babe God,] for after he announced to the shepherds, *To you has been born a Saviour*, (he continued,) *who is the Lord Christ*[24].

Therefore all the things which were said by Simeon are truly congruous with the babe Jesus who is God in his nature. And even if the hearing of the words falls short of their meaning and the sight of the babe (falls short) of faith upon him—for it is written that even *Joseph and Mary were amazed at the things which were spoken about him*[25]—and he (—Simeon—) did not say that they were said about him or affirmed with God for him, nevertheless (he it is) about whom they were said and to whom they adhere and of whom they are. And he is God, who was being blessed by Simeon and whom he was petitioning to release him from life. And it is clear (that it is) because he fore-bound him to life (that)—for *Release thou thy servant, my Lord, according to thy word in peace*[26] shows this—as him from whom he has fore-heard something he makes mention of him. *Behold, mine eyes have seen thy favour*[27]—this (means), *I have seen thy corporality, by which thou hast saved the world.* For this he called *favour* because all spiritual benefits, which *eye has not seen and ear has not heard*[28], according to the word of Paul, have been prepared for men by the corporality of God. And the priest said these things, he marvelling

[20] *Lk.* 1,*72.* [21] Cf. *Is.* 42,*6*; 49,*6.* [22] *Lk.* 1,*76-77.* [23] *Mt.* 1,*21.* [24] *Lk.* 2,*11.*
[25] *Ibid.*, *33.* [26] *Ibid.*, *29.* [27] *Ibid.*, *30.* [28] *1 Cor.* 2,*9.*

more than anyone, (he) who divinely and spiritually received from him the revelation that he would remain alive.

Therefore after Simeon said these great things unto Jesus, he blessed Joseph and Mary his mother, as he petitioned him as (one does) God and blessed them as (one does) men. And he gave to them the blessing of which they who become ministers of this mystery have been made
* p. 44 worthy. * And because Mary marvelled at the things which she heard about her son, Simeon said to her, *(It is) not ye only (who) are amazed at him and variously take opinions about him, but everyone will marvel at him, and many will fall and others rise through him.* That is, *Behold, he is set for the falling and for the rising of many in Israel*[29]. For he is, Jesus, *a sign of contention*[30], against whom all tongues speak and by whom all of them are conquered, and whose greatness while contending against him they proclaim. For this sign which is placed in the middle teaches the two things, and that they who believe understand that it shows such things and do not fall into debates and conflicts, but those who do not believe fall into contentions against one another.

And Simeon, extending his word and making known the more the incomprehensibility of Christ, said to Mary, *Even through your own soul the spear will pass*[31]. That is, *(At this moment) not to others he becomes a sign of contention, but indeed to you, for you do not recognise him as he is, but as you are able you think about him. And (that is) not as he deserves to be believed, for if you had believed in him as is right, you would not have been amazed with my words at (the fact) that I called him God, who has authority over life and over death.* And well did he call this defective opinion which Mary had a spear and say that it would pass through her soul, because she did not remain until the end in this understanding which is not adequate to Christ, but she learnt through the coming of the Holy Spirit — she with the apostles — about the greatness of him to whom she gave birth. But this word, *Through your own soul the spear will pass*[32], makes known two considerations. One (is) this which has been said, and the other (is) that she too with the apostles would be offended at him, for she too
* p. 45 is included in * the meaning of that cry, *All of you will be offended at me this night*[33]. Therefore he called that offence which came about after a short time a spear which would pass through her, and he made

[29] *Lk.* 2,34. [30] *Ibid.* [31] *Lk.* 2,35. [32] *Ibid.* [33] *Mt.* 26,31; *Mk.* 14,27.

known their weakness and that opinion which she had that it was not adequate to Christ. Because she did not know at the time that she brought him to the temple that she was offering the only Son of God, embodied, before his Father, but as every mother is accustomed to bring her first-born (so did she), she too *brought up him* to whom she gave birth *that* she *might present him before* God[34]. And that Mary did not have at that time faith which is adequate to Jesus her rebuke to him shows — *My son, why have you done to us so? For behold, I and your father in great anxiety have been seeking you*[35] — who to this word which is not appropriate to him said, *Do you not know that I must be in my Father's house?*[36] It is written that *they did not understand the word which he spoke to them*[37], and it is clear that (they did not understand it) because they were not persuaded that he was the true Son of God. Therefore two things, as I have said, Simeon makes known in his word : the offence of Mary and the defectiveness of her faith. And because both of them received correction, for she was to recognise him true God and also the offence which she took would be swiftly healed, he says to her, *Through your own soul the spear will pass*[38].

But that he said, *That thoughts of the hearts of many may be revealed*[39], makes known this : *If you who conceived him and gave birth to him do not yet know him, who is (there) who knows him now, what he is?* And the word is said against them who at that time and now reckon him a man and against these who run after his incomprehensibility, for the thoughts of all who are not worthy of him and do not as it is right that he be believed God believe in him are revealed and made known. Nevertheless they who take offence from weakness, like Mary, receive corrections * from grace like her; others who from an evil will blaspheme, * p. 46
as (did) indeed the Jews at that time, are placed in their number. Therefore indeed this is made known the meaning in *that thoughts of hearts may be revealed.* As one says, that *spear* which *passes through your soul* — this is *the doubt and the offence which pass through you* — (they) clearly reveal *the thoughts of the hearts* of everyone whether from weakness or from evil they doubt or are offended, which has been seen in fact with many. Therefore in the things which were said by Simeon about the doubt of Mary we have learnt these and such things, and *thoughts of many hearts* have been made known to us,

[34] Cf. *Lk.* 2,22. [35] *Ibid., 48.* [36] *Ibid., 49.* [37] *Ibid., 50.* [38] *Ibid., 35.* [39] *Ibid.*

(the many) against whom (also) applies that word of the apostle (in) which he said, *His judgements may not be searched and his ways may not be fathomed*[40].

But Joseph and Mary, *when* they heard these things from Simeon and *they completed everything as* it is commanded *in the law, returned to Nazareth, their city*[41], simply and innocently serving the divine economy.

For[42] this day the temple entered the temple. The temple which (is) the body of Christ (is) what entered the Jerusalem temple. The temple of God the Word, who (is) in union with the one, this day made entry into (the other,) the temple of Jerusalem. And he who receives sacrifices and offerings from all offered this day a sacrifice. And he who bears all in his power was borne this day in the arms of old Simeon. And he petitioned him who appeared an infant and a babe now to release him in peace. And he calls the infant Lord and the babe God, and petitions that he might have favour upon him saying, *For behold, mine eyes have seen thy great favour which thou hast prepared in the face of all peoples. Release me, my Lord, in peace, because my soul has been satisfied by thy appearance. Now release me, because thou hast* * p. 47 *gladdened me by thy appearance. Therefore thou art * the Christ of the Lord*[43], *therefore thou art the hope of Jacob and the confidence of Israel, thou art the light of the nations and glory to thy people, thou art the expectation of all. Now release me, because behold, mine eyes have seen the hope which ages and generations expect. Release me, because thou hast bound me to life that I may be made worthy to thy divine appearance. I confess to thee that thou hast fashioned for me hands that I may bear thee, my Lord, thee who bearest all. Glory (be) to thee, who hast placed in me breath and bound me to life until the revelation of thy coming to the world. Glory (be) to thee, who hast made me worthy that I may see thy glory. Now release me in peace at this time, for I have seen thee, the light of the nations and the glory of Israel. Thou, my Lord, givest life and breath to all, and thou hast bound me that I may not taste death until I see thee in this life. Now thou hast fulfilled with thy servant thy promise. Now release me in peace from this life, for behold, mine eyes have seen thy favour*[44].

[40] *Rom.* 11,*33*. [41] *Lk.* 2,*39*. [42] As DE HALLEUX, *Philoxène*, p. 144, n. 7 has observed, the concluding paragraph of this fragment appears to be a homiletic addition to the text of Philoxenus "to be read at the feast of the ὑπάντησις" (cf. the title). [43] *Lk.* 2,*26*. [44] Cf. *ibid.*, *29-32*.

Also Anna the old prophetess has been made worthy of thy divine appearance. And *she came up at that very hour and* praised *the Lord and spoke* by the Holy Spirit *about*[45] the Saviour who was revealed in her days and gives release from wearisome life to the old, for he is our God, as it is written[46]. With Simeon let us bear his body in our hands from the holy altar and with him let us ask not that he might release us from life only, but that he might release us from the bonds of sin, not that we might see him with bodily eyes, but that in our heart we might bear him night and day and on him fix the mind of our thoughts, that in his appearance we may take delight in this life in the mystery and in the new world in the fullness of sight and deed. And before the throne of his greatness let us render confession of his love towards us, for he has made us worthy to this extent, that we should become sons and inheritors of his great things. And there may ascend to him glory, and to his Father and to the Holy Spirit, now and always and unto age of ages, Amen.

Fragment 44. Luke 2,40 p. 48

... *to the souls* of sinners *which had been held in Sheol*[1], because it is written that *the souls of the righteous are in the hands of God*[2], where he previously committed their lives when they were in the body. But the souls of sinners remain in Sheol with the body, and because (the sinners) loved the [satisfactions] and the pleasures of the body, (their souls) remain with it in corruption, not in it but with it. But the souls of the wicked who have renounced God or (the souls) which have not believed God at all are in the hands of the demons.

Therefore [in] his body which was placed within the tomb *he preached* [also] *to the souls*[3] of sinners, and it is clear [that (it was) not] a dead body (which) was proclaiming [the resurrection]. Because a dead body is only of sinners and of the wicked, how much more the body of God may be confessed to be a living (body) and to give life. But even today human life departs from the bodies of the righteous, yet that the divine life does not abandon them testify the signs which happened upon their bones and the demons who cry out and teach about the

[45] *Ibid., 38*. [46] Cf. *Ps*. 68,*20*?

Fr. 44 [1] *1 Pet*. 3,*19*. [2] *Wisdom* 3,*1*. [3] Cf. above, n. 1.

divine life that it has remained with them. And if thus (it is) with the righteous servants, with the Lord God how much the more.

So then well it is said that the Spirit, who embodied Jesus, was marvellously joined to his body, [*in*] *whom* [Luke] said [he who *was growing*] *in his stature* also *was becoming strong*[4]. And he was setting the ages for the growth of his stature which (came) afterwards, in order that everyone who is born by the Spirit from water may grow in this stature, if worldly [pleasures], as I have said, do not bring to an end his growth. And justly these things are written about Jesus, because the head of another race he became to us, and in place of the Adam who (is) from dust the Adam who (is) from heaven was made known[5] [to us. And] the first Adam, who (is) from
* p. 49 dust, [after * the Holy Spirit] departed from him [because of the transgression of the commandment], had no [growth of] spiritual stature[6], for how could he have [grown] in that which once he [caused to go out] from him? Nor *was he filled with* [*wisdom*][6], for [wisdom does not remain] where evil enters[7]. [Nor], furthermore, *was the grace of God upon him*[6], that which made him a beloved (one) and a pleasing (one) [to natures] and to races, by which *he called names* [*to*] *all*[8] and received authority over everything and by which he became also the likeness and the image of God[9]. And as to the likeness of God all races and natures without reason were subjected to him, that immediately it departed from him everything rebelled against him and in place of authority...

FRAGMENT 45. LUKE 2,42-49

... the age of twelve years for this manner of life. For if it is not too small [for] human [thoughts], how is it inadequate for divine thoughts? And if many at this age are brought to the association of [marriage], how should they not be capable that association without corruption with the Holy Spirit should become to them, that (association) which also Jesus [manifested]? As he *grew and became strong in*[1] it,

[4] *Lk.* 2,*40*; *52*. [5] Cf. *1 Cor.* 15,*45*; *47*. [6] *Lk.* 2,*40*. [7] Cf. *Wisdom* 1,*4*?
[8] *Gen.* 2,*20*. [9] Cf. *ibid.* 1,*26*; etc.
Fr. 45 [1] *Lk.* 2,*40*.

he manifested the fruit of his [growth] and chose to be in the [temple] of God and to be pupil and questioner to the doctors.

For the evangelist did not simply make known in this place what was the age of Jesus, but that the common doctrine comes through him to everyone and he shows that from here it is right for men that they should [begin] choosing the virtues. But for Jesus (himself) this age was not the beginning of good works, because anything against the good was never set in motion in him, * neither passion nor thought, but what was in him and had not been made known he made known here in deed, for he remained in the temple of God, being constant in the study of doctrine. For even if men receive the doctrine of the world until this age, yet there are who [are complete in] it seven year olds and others ... olds — and how many times (is it) less than these? — because they learn the human voice only and the composed word. But from the age of twelve years and above a man is indeed able to receive also divine thoughts, to hear and to speak words which are not composed and to attain to the sight of spiritual wisdom, which (is) above the world, that which as it seems to me was given in [the economy even] to John the Baptist. Because [he was driven out] by the Holy Spirit [into the wilderness][2] he grew there[3], and with growth of stature his soul also increased in divine thoughts. And this, which we have not known in John because his growth in spiritual things has not been written down, we have come to know in the growth of Christ.

* p. 50

And no one will think much of the word, which is not on the level of persuasion, while he looks to the things which grow within the world, for in the world there are many things which hinder man that he might not come to the sensation of spiritual things. For how may he sense that in which he does not grow, seeing that it is clear that the manner of life of men is a dense and corporeal (one), not only on account of food and drink, but also by human satisfactions and by the sights which set in motion lusts? And even if they who grow in the stature of childhood are not in these things, nevertheless (the things) come to them, because all the dealing of the world and human ways of life lead to lusts, harden the mind and darken the thoughts. And although in the time of his infancy a man does not sense lusts because they are asleep in him, when [he has] reached the

[2] Cf. *Mt.* 4,*1*; *Mk.* 1,*12*; *Lk.* 4,*1*? [3] Cf. *Lk.* 1,*80*?

age of childhood they are aroused in him, even when he may not will * p. 51 (it), and they excite * the members and stir thoughts. And he whose growth and dealing is this is not able to sense spiritual things at the age of twelve years, but only the things into which he has grown and (to which) he has become accustomed.

But with Jesus (it is) the opposite, for because lust was not implanted in his embodying dealings from outside did not become for it fostering agents and human sights did not arouse it. But at this age of twelve years he made known to everyone what manner was the hidden growth of his thoughts and he set through this a limit for them who would receive his Spirit and become his members. However these first come to know the evil and then the good, because first the lust of the body is set in motion in men and then after [it] are found doctors and instructors and the good growth of the desire of the Spirit. But in Jesus (it is) not so, but the desire and the choice of the good was prior, which at this age which is written was revealed, and not after he rejected the evil did he choose the good, for how could he have rejected what he altogether did not know? As it is written, *Before the child will know to reject the evil he will choose the good*[4]. Therefore Jesus did not reject and then choose but showed openly what (it) was which was prior and chosen by him, and he delivered the common doctrine to all who are in this stature that from here they might reject the evil things and choose the good things and exchange the dealing of the world for the dealing which (is) with God. And they may not lay hold of a pretext in lack of days and fewness of years, for, as has been said once, everything which is of the world or of thought or of association or of other bodily satisfaction this stature is found to serve, so then the more (should it serve) those which are spiritual (things)[5].

But there are some who have supposed concerning the first Adam that at this age of twelve years...

p. 52

FRAGMENT 46. LUKE 2,51-52

...from these things which we have said, but also from the whole writing of the gospel. But Luke adds to *he went down to Nazareth*

[4] *Is.* 7,*16*. [5] Cf. above, p. 42,*26-31*.

and he was obedient to them that *his mother kept all the words in her heart*[1], and it is clear that (she did so) because they were not of nature or of custom. But in another place it is written, *She kept and compared all the words*[2], and further, *But Joseph and his mother were amazed at the things which were said about him*[3], at which, if they had not seen that they were new and strange, they would not have been amazed. And furthermore, Mary would not have kept and compared them one with another, for if they had been natural as of everyone, she would not have needed to compare them. But comparing the words which (were spoken) about him and the deeds which (happened) to him with themselves and with the rest of other men, she marvelled at these of Jesus as at new ones, because not even to her had yet been made known the peculiarity of the mystery, which was revealed after the coming of the Spirit, for *the Holy Spirit had not been given because Jesus had not yet been glorified*[4]. And that she had conceived and given birth without marriage Mary knew, but that she had given birth to God, who was embodied and became from her man, she was not persuaded of, because (it was) not sensibly (that) he was embodied from her but as by wonder, she not knowing. This (is a thing) which is common also to these who conceive from seed, that while the conception is being fashioned and formed in them they do not sense (it), and if with nature (it is) thus, how much more are these things of the economy known above word, thought and sensation. And because she did not know clearly at that time that she had given birth to God embodied, she marvelled at the things which she saw in him and heard from the rest of others about him.

And after the evangelist has narrated these things which happened through him * and to him and by him up to twelve years, he gathers up all of them, the former and the latter, and says that *Jesus grew in stature and in wisdom and in grace with God and men*[5]. But above he said that *the child grew and became strong in spirit*[6], and here that *Jesus grew in wisdom and stature*[7], to show that from this age and above he no longer knows him (as) a child. But from seven and up to twelve years he is thus known, and from this age and above (is) another order of stature. With that (there is) the other (fact), that he did not write here that *he grew and became strong in spirit*[8], but that *he grew in stature*[9] ...

* p. 53

Fr. 46 [1] *Lk.* 2,51. [2] *Ibid.*, 19. [3] *Ibid.*, 33. [4] *Jn.* 7,39. [5] *Lk.* 2,52. [6] *Ibid.*, 40. [7] Cf. above, n. 5. [8] Cf. above, n. 6. [9] Cf. above, n. 5.

FRAGMENT 47. LUKE 2,51-52[1]

The evangelist Luke shows what things came about by Christ and to him and for him and about him. By him : as *he went up every year to the temple*[2]; and his questions to the doctors[3]; and his speaking with Mary[4]; and his obedience to his parents by grace[5]. But to him : as *he was circumcised*[6]; and *he was wrapped in swaddling clothes and he was laid in a manger*[7]. But for him : as *they took him up to the temple and presented him before the Lord*[8]; and they offered for him offerings[9]. And about him, furthermore : these things which were spoken by Zechariah and Elizabeth, and the angels and the shepherds, and Simeon and Anna[10].

FRAGMENT 48. LUKE 2,52

* p. 54 ...*that the weakness of God is stronger than men* * *and his foolishness is wiser than men*[1]. And if his weakness is stronger than the strength of men it is not grasped by them, and his foolishness is not known by their wisdom, for the great things of rational (beings) are not able to understand the lowly things of God. And if this (fact) that he grew in his stature is reckoned by you [weakness], and that he increased in his wisdom (is reckoned by you) lack, look, the apostle said that they are not grasped by men. Therefore it is sufficient for you to know who is he who grew and you should not seek how. Namely, *Jesus grew in stature and in wisdom and in grace*[2], and that Jesus is Christ I suppose is believed by you, and that *Christ is the power of God and his wisdom*[3], behold, Paul cries out to you. Therefore the power grew in stature and the wisdom, it (grew) in itself. Namely, *the Holy Spirit will come and the power of the Most High will cover you*[4]; and *the power* who *covered*, he was embodied; and he who was embodied weak flesh and received a rational soul, he grew in both of them, in the stature of his body and in the wisdom of his soul. And if we are not able to understand the mystery of his growth we do

Fr. 47 [1] **Title** : Of the holy Mar Xenaias of Mabbug, from the thirty-fifth chapter against the Nestorians. Commentary of these things which are set down below. [2] *Lk.* 2,41 (cf. *ibid.*, 22). [3] Cf. *ibid.*, 46. [4] Cf. *ibid.*, 49. [5] Cf. *ibid.*, 51. [6] *Ibid.*, 21. [7] *Ibid.*, 7. [8] *Ibid.*, 22. [9] Cf. *ibid.*, 24. [10] Cf. *Lk.* 1-2.

Fr. 48 [1] *1 Cor.* 1,25. [2] *Lk.* 2,52. [3] *1 Cor.* 1,24. [4] *Lk.* 1,35.

not marvel, for of God are these things which are not explained, and not of man.

And if his great things may not be investigated, how may his lowly things be examined?—for perhaps easier it is that the great things of God be spoken than that his lowly things be grasped, for his great things are of his nature but his lowly things of the wonder which happened in his hypostasis. And if this (fact) that God became low is a wonder, all things which are connected to it are also wonders. And it is not possible that wonders be explained, but (they are) to lead the mind to be astonished and to wonder at them, not only these things which happened in God but also the others which he did in the rest of the (created) works. And if the signs which happened in the (created) works are not grasped — not what befell Egypt, and not what he did in the wilderness, and not what things happened in all generations, and not these things which Jesus showed in things outside of himself, and not the things which are [performed] in natures and in bodies from the beginning of the world * and up to with us and are * p. 55 supposed of custom — how may a man seek to grasp and to explain the wonder which newly happened in the hypostasis of the Word, that he *was emptied*[5] and became man and fulfilled in his becoming all things of men? As I think, not rational and to be thought nothing of (is) he who [attends] to these things, because he has not previously recognised what they are and whose, these things which are being examined by him.

Therefore if it is written that Jesus grew, and Jesus is God the Word as…

Fragment 49. Luke 2,52

…but with him who by his will was emptied[1] and became man. And furthermore, (that *with God* was) to set for us the goal that first with God we should grow in good things, and then with men. And furthermore, that *with God* (was) in order that he might become as the Father, since he became inferior to him because he became man. And furthermore, that men did not have this, that they may grow

[5] Cf. *Phil.* 2,7.
Fr. 49 [1] Cf. *Phil.* 2,7.

perfectly with God, except in parts with a few righteous ones and prophets, (that also was why) he first grew and prepared a way, that everyone may grow as he wills and as far as he wills, and even attain to *that they may be one in us*[2]. But if a man wishes to understand the word according to its exterior and says that because he became man he grew first with God in good things and then with men, neither (is) this far from the truth.

But in connection with the heretics who say that he who grew in stature and increased in wisdom and in grace was an ordinary man as one of us, I wish to use here a few words and ask them first who they say that Jesus is: a natural man, or God and a man? And if they say the former, let them attend to the Scriptures, which everywhere call Jesus God, and the equal[3] and the consubstantial[4] of the
* p. 56 Father, and the maker of the ages[5] * and he who is before all[6], for from here either a man is to be considered to be the equal of God and the maker of all, or ours stands: that Jesus is God the Word. And as of the Son by nature the Scriptures speak of him, but from whom do they say that the man received wisdom and grace? If from the Father, look, then he is the Son. And if from the Son, Jesus is not the Son of God. Or if from the Holy Spirit, as one of the prophets, why is he Son and they prophets? Or if from the Trinity he was instructed and received grace, he is to be reckoned as one of the servants, all of whom were created by the divine nature and by it are constituted and sustained.

But if he as a son by grace increased more than everyone, of which of the hypostases is he to be reckoned son? If they say of the Father, because the name *son* fits with *Father*, then who is of God the Word? Or if he is considered son of the Father and of the Son and of the Spirit together, then all of the divine nature should be called Father, and where (then) is what is known of the hypostases and the variety of names? But if they say that the divine nature is the Father of men, following the foolish thought of Theodore, this is of his opinion and (is) not the doctrine of the [Scriptures], which everywhere name Father the one hypostasis who truly begot one Son without beginning. And to him he is reckoned the natural Father, and to us, the baptised, (Father) by grace because we have become brothers to the natural Son

[2] *Jn.* 17,*21*. [3] Cf. *Phil.* 2,*6*? [4] Cf. *Heb.* 1,*3*? [5] Cf. *Col.* 1,*16*? *1 Tim.* 1,*17*?
[6] Cf. *Col.* 1,*17*?

by baptism, (we) who from here are called brothers of the Son and sons of the Father. As was said by the Son to his Father, *I will proclaim thy name to my brothers*[7]. And further, *He was not ashamed to call them his brothers*[8]. Therefore we are brothers of the natural Son and sons of God the Father, and (it is) not (true that) because Father, Son and Spirit are believed one nature the term *Fatherhood* is (a term) of nature, as indeed the embodying and the birth from the virgin and the suffering * and death are not common (to each of them) because * p. 57
they are one essence.

But if from that of the Jews they give an example also to our adoption and as with them the (divine) nature and not the hypostasis of the Father was reckoned Father they suppose (it to be) so also with us, they reject the economy of the Father, deny the salvation of the Son and reckon our goods to be like those of the Jews. For theirs, the adoption with them, was a type, and all their goods were shadows which hasten towards the body. And ours are the body and the reality[9], for not outside the hypostasis of the Son are we known sons, but he is the head and we members in his body. And on this account he became man, to make us sons of God, and as his incorporation was not of name only but of true deed, so too that he made us his members and sons of his Father is not of word only, as with the Jews. (In) that far one he did not become man and so did not make sons, he was not brought low and so did not exalt, he did not accept shame and so did not give honour. But as he gave to Moses the name of God[10], so he gave to Israel the appellation of son and sent word to Pharaoh through Moses, wishing to give honour to the people before its enemies, *Send to me my son, my first-born, Israel, and he shall serve me*[11]. And while to Pharaoh he was making known the honour of the people, to Moses he was showing its rejection and the election of others, for he did not simply call it son, but he added *first-born*, which teaches that others would enter after it. And the word was a sign to Moses that as Ishmael and Esau and Reuben were rejected and others entered in their place, he would cast out Israel and the Gentiles would be received in its place. And if from the start of its election its expulsion was made known, how can its sonship be compared with ours?

[7] *Ps.* 22,*23*; *Heb.* 2,*12*. [8] *Heb.* 2,*11*. [9] Cf. *Col.* 2,*17*; *Heb.* 8,*5*; 10,*1*. [10] Cf. *Ex.* 3,*13-15*. [11] *Ibid.* 4,*23* (cf. *22*).

Because, therefore, in name only the first people was honoured, it was reckoned son of God. But this is of the divine nature, and not
* p. 58 of the hypostasis of the Father, for neither Father * nor Son nor Spirit had been made known to them to whom everywhere the doctrine concerning the nature was delivered, in the saying that *God is one*[12]. But here, seeing that with the faith in the nature the confession of the hypostases has also been revealed, rightly sons of the hypostasis of the Father are [reckoned] these who have been elected to the honour of adoption, who have not simply received the name (of sons), but because they have become brothers by grace to the natural Son — and this, furthermore, did not happen simply in word without deed, but the Son first became man and then made men sons — are also born anew and so become (sons). That is, *You were buried with him by baptism into death, and through it*[13] *you have risen with him*[14]. And the apostle further said, *Do you not know that we who have been baptised into Jesus Christ have been baptised into his death? You were buried with him by baptism into death, so that as Jesus Christ rose from the dead by the glory of his Father, we too might likewise walk in new life*[15]. For we have become immortals and so sons, since it was not right that dead persons should become members in the living body of Christ. And that God does not accept that those who are subject to death should become to him sons and friends, but those who are the living and the immortals in his likeness — his words testify. And about the friends he said, "*I am the God of Abraham and of Isaac and of Jacob*". *And he is not God of the dead, but of the living; for all of them live to him*[16]. And about the sons he further proclaims through the prophet, *I have said that you are gods and sons of the Most High, all of you. Henceforward as any man you will die*[17]. And he showed that mortal men are not sons, and those who are made worthy of the honour of sons are immortals.

So then neither ordinary men nor angels are reckoned by the Scriptures sons of God, but only those who become from men sons through death and resurrection. And because they have become
* p. 59 brothers to the Son who became man by the new birth * from baptism, they are necessarily also recognised sons of the Father, for if the deed

[12] *Deut.* 6,*4*; *Mk.* 12,*29*. [13] *I.e.*: death. Or: him. [14] *Col.* 2,*12*; cf. *Rom.* 6,*4*. [15] *Rom.* 6,*3-4*; cf. *Col.* 2,*12*. [16] *Mt.* 22,*32*; *Mk.* 12,*26-27*; *Lk.* 20,*37-38*. [17] *Ps.* 82,*6-7*.

of brotherhood is common (to both), the name of fatherhood is also of both, of the head and of his members, of the Word who became man and of the men who became sons. And as we are truly born men from the natural womb, in truth and in fact we also become sons from the womb of baptism. And the first is instructive about this second in that that one is no false (one) and this one no metaphorical (one).

There is then no place for your new and strange thought that the divine nature is to be reckoned the Father of man, or (that) these who receive the honour of adoption become sons of the (divine) nature, and not of the hypostasis of the Father. And the metaphorical adoption with the Jews is not adequate to become an example for our honour, for there there came only the word: *I have said that you are gods and sons of the Most High*[18]. *I have said*, the word is written, and not *I have made*. He said and he promised, but he did not make. But here he promised before the foundations of the world and fulfilled his promise in the fullness of the times, for *he chose you in him from before the foundations of the world*[19]. And furthermore, Jesus said to his disciples, *You had been chosen by me from before the foundations of the world*[20].

But if the heretic should say that all believers are sons of the hypostasis of the Father, with that man he may be asked who gave this honour and from where and how it was received. And if from baptism, which is a type of death and resurrection, the baptised have received it, as the apostle teaches, from where did that man get it? To say by his own death and resurrection—that has no order, as indeed men by their death and resurrection have not been made equal to it. But then the death and resurrection of others—it is reckoned that when a man participates in them he may become a son. And it is found that God the Word has been tempted by these[21], through participation with whose suffering and resurrection man has been made equal * to whose honour. And while the heretic removes God from sufferings, the more to sufferings does he subject him, because he is found (to say) that he was not embodied nor born bodily and so did not suffer, he who takes away this birth for man. * p. 60

And if, furthermore, he flees from reckoning Jesus only a man and

[18] *Ibid.* [19] *Eph.* 1,*4*. [20] *Jn.* 15,*16*? *Jn.* 17,*24*? *2 Thess.* 2,*13*? [21] Cf. *Heb.* 2,*18*; 4,*15*.

confesses him cunningly, according to his custom, God and a man, we may ask him which of the two of them grew. And if he says that the growth was common, because it is written that *Jesus grew*[22], so also God is found a deficient. And if only he grew, or if (the growth occured only) with an other man, in each one of them (he who grew) is known not to be Christ. With that (there is) another (fact), that first it is written about him that *he grew in stature*[22], and if he was not embodied and did not become man, how did he grow? Look, we indeed who believe that these words are written about God first confess that he became and he took the origin of man, and therefore we place growth upon him. But you say that he grew in association with a man, as God who is not embodied, which is clearly blasphemy. And furthermore, in that it is not written that they grew, but that *Jesus grew*[22], and the evangelist made known lucidly that the growth was singular, whether he should be reckoned a man or God, then what Jesus is called by you, *God and a man*, is an empty and false word, uttered as a deception which (deceives only) the simple as the rascality of the doctrine may not be hidden; for from here Jesus may be known to be either God embodied, as we believe, or a righteous man, as Theodore and Nestorius understand, and this *God and a man* which has newly been found by the heretics is senseless.

And if they are relying on (the fact) that this expression is said in the writings of the Fathers, let them first believe like them that God
* p. 61 became man without change. And then they may use * their word, for by that *God and man* they did not understand "one and another", but (they used it) to teach that (God) was truly embodied, and his divinity was not changed in his embodying nor his corporality destroyed or dissolved after he was embodied. But as he is believed God in that which he is, also is he confessed man in this which he has become, and a change in either of them did not occur. And if this is their meaning, different (is) your contrary (one), which confesses only the conjunction and the association of name of God and of a man.

Their word is not like yours, for you unite not the natures but the properties which they have. And you proclaim that a man participated in the great things of God, but deny that God the Word was joined with the lowly things of man, and you follow senselessly the stupid word of Nestorius, which proclaims two natures. And furthermore,

[22] *Lk.* 2,52.

he says (there was) to them one power, one will, one wisdom and one authority [23]. And if he so understands, it was necessary that each one of the natures should have these which were united, (namely) power, wisdom and authority. And what was, then, the power, wisdom and authority of the man? And if he did not possess any of these, for for this reason he would have been assumed by God, that he might participate in things which he did not have, (then it is) not (the case that) the actions of the two of them were one, but the man would have been joined to the great things of God. And if this stands and they became one wisdom, how could Jesus have grown in wisdom? And if they were one authority, how could he have increased in grace? And if they became one power, where is *the weakness of God is stronger than men* [24], for God, as you say, did not participate in weakness and the man, who possessed [it] naturally, became one power with God? Where then is *the weakness of God is stronger than men*[24], for if * the weakness is not first acknowledged, neither is it clear that (it is) stronger? And while you remove God from lowly things, the more do you seize him from great things. And again, if the two of them became one wisdom, how could Jesus have grown in wisdom? If he who increased was a man, they did not become [one] wisdom as you say. And if the growth is of both of them, God is found one who does not know and even he would have needed to grow because he is not complete. And where is the wisdom of God in which the man participated, for look, even it would have been found and gained in growth? Either, therefore, they did not become one wisdom as you say, or if they did become (one wisdom), Jesus did not grow in wisdom. For in what wisdom would he have grown, he who participated once in God the Word and was made known with him one wisdom? * p. 62

Where, when and how is it possible that the wisdom of God and of a man should become one? Did that of the man increase and become equal with [that of] God, or did that of God decrease and become measured with that of the man? With that (there is) another (question): when and where did the wisdom of that man become known and then become one with that of God? If they say that the unification became in the womb, how may there become wisdom to him who has not yet become a son? And if he was united to God at his very creation and the two of them became one, how is it written that *Jesus grew in*

[23] Cf. Loofs, *Nestoriana*, pp. 196, *15-17*; 224, *12-15*; etc. [24] *1 Cor.* 1,*25*.

stature and in wisdom[25]? And if when he was twelve years old, after this number it is written that *he grew*[25]. But if he became one wisdom (with God) in baptism, after it there is said, *That day and that hour man does not know, neither the angels nor the Son*[26]. And if the man does not know the hour of his coming, for you understand *the Son* in that place (as referring) to him, how could he have become one wisdom with God? But if this [association] became after the resur-
* p. 63 rection, where * he said, *All authority in heaven and on earth has been given to me*[27], how could he have said to his disciples at the time of his ascension, when *they asked him, "At*[28] *this time will you restore the kingdom to Israel?", "It has not become yours to know the time or the times which the Father has set by the authority of himself"*[29], and shown that these things [are known] to the Father alone? And if they became one wisdom and one authority after he was taken up, why did Paul say, *Christ died and rose and is at the right hand of God and seeks for us*[30]? How does he seek as one in need if they became one authority? And the more, in that Paul said that Christ seeks, whom you interpret to be God and a man, therefore both of them together are seeking from the Father. But if (he is) only a man, he did not become one authority and one power with the Word. And if a place has not been found among all these in which it is said that God and a man became one authority, power and wisdom, then there are not two as you think, and the association which you proclaim did not become, but Christ, God's power and his wisdom[31], was emptied[32] by the will of the Father and became without change weak man.

And as it fitted his body that it should grow in stature, so also his soul that it should increase in wisdom and his weakness that it should receive grace. And while he was seen a weak (one), he was made known a strong (one). And while wisdom was being increased to him, the more the economy of his wisdom was revealed. And these things are believed because they are written, and not because they are understood by their hearers. For the economy of God is an ineffable mystery, and we are not ashamed to confess that our doctrine is not understood or explained, but in this do we [the more] boast, that we lay hold of a mystery which may not be comprehended by knowledge. And while all wisdoms and all doctrines may be investigated and

[25] *Lk.* 2,*52*. [26] *Mk.* 13,*32*. [27] *Mt.* 28,*18*. [28] Lit.: If (*rendering of* εἰ, *Acts* 1,*6*) at.
[29] *Acts* 1,*6-7*. [30] *Rom.* 8,*34*. [31] Cf. *1 Cor.* 1,*24*. [32] Cf. *Phil.* 2,*7*.

understood, these things of ours remain * in silence. They are only to * p. 64 be believed, because they are not to be understood. And by the lost they are reckoned folly; and by believers, ineffable wisdom. For *the word of the cross is folly to the lost*[33]; and by the name *cross* it is clear that he indicated the entire economy, in that first the birth from a virgin is reckoned folly by the lost, seeing that they do not believe that God dwelt in the womb and was embodied man and was born of woman. Both heathen and Jews totally deny the (virgin) birth and do not believe that Jesus was born of a virgin. And heretics, who are thought to accept the confession of the mystery, grant it to a man instead of God and say that a natural babe was conceived without marriage and born without seed. And by another path they go out to what is said by Jews and heathen, in that if he who was conceived and born is not God, and a natural man does not become without marriage, they both think about that (birth by) which he was born of Mary as the Jews and the heathen (do) and like them confine him (to being) a natural man. And in this the blasphemy is only changed, for that of those (heathen and Jews) is spoken openly and theirs is veiled with cunning. For truly (it is) that it does not accord with the order of nature that God should become man and be born of woman, that with it this does not fit. And the nature of men is not adequate for it, (for this miracle), and as much as human thought may gaze upon it, upon the miracle, (the miracle) escapes from it. Yet Christians, who believe not because they understand it but because it is written, accept it, and making a comparison of the act with the power of God attribute it to his might, remembering the word of the messenger of the mystery that *nothing is difficult for God*[34].

But if, furthermore, the heretic still disputes and says, *How is it possible that God should grow in stature and in wisdom, he who is perfect and complete in his being?* we reply to him that Paul called Christ the power and the wisdom of God[35], and it is known that the Son is the power and wisdom of the Father. * Therefore Christ is the Son of God. * p. 65 And because it is written that Jesus grew, but Jesus is Christ, the Son of God is he who grew in stature and in wisdom. And if he says that God the Word is the power and wisdom of the Father, he is found to confess that Christ is God the Word. And if God the Word is Christ, but Jesus is Christ, these things which are written adhere to God the

[33] *1 Cor.* 1,*18*. [34] *Lk.* 1,*37*. [35] Cf. *1 Cor.* 1,*24*.

Word. And where salvation had been made ready for men and renewal and fulfilment for everything which has become, he was called Saviour by fact. But if he says that metaphorically Christ is called God the Word, then also (is he so called) man, and if both of them (are done) metaphorically, where is genuine man? For look, it is known that Jesus, who by you is considered a man, is Christ and God the Word. Now *Jesus grew in stature and in wisdom*[36], and if he grew in stature, it is clear that where he does not have stature he does not have growth, and where he does not have a human soul he does not receive increase of wisdom. Therefore grasp the bodily beginning and join to it the human facts, and may you not take offence at the way of the economy, nor treating alike his nature with his economy and his divine things with his human things, deny the common salvation[37]! Stature, therefore, is of the body and corporality became to him from Mary, and from there he received a human soul. And from where he began in the growth of stature, he also began in the increase of wisdom. And he who says that wisdom was not increased to him manifestly denies also the growth of stature and with this also his genuine corporality, and he is made known a disciple not only of Paul of Samosata and of Sabellius, but even more of Mani and of Marcion, for they reject the corporality of God and his economy for our salvation.

Therefore Jesus grew in these things which are written about him, first in the stature of his body, and according to his ages also in
* p. 66 wisdom, and with this also in the grace of God. And as * the ages of his stature sprung up one out of another, so also did his wisdom grow out of [itself]. And growing was made known by appearance and by other things connected to it, wisdom by learning and grace by signs and miracles. And if it is not written that miracles happened before the baptism, (that is) because he loved men and was beloved by them —as *Joseph found favour*[38] *before his lord*[39] and also *in the sight of the governor of the prison*[40], and as *he found favour before Pharaoh*[41], and as *the apostles had found favour*[38] *before the whole people*[42].

But about that *with God*[43], we have said *he grew also* in part above. And if we are not able to write about it exactly, that is not to be wondered at, because indeed these things which are held to be revealed are not *known* by us, and not every spiritual sight comes to word and

[36] *Lk.* 2,52. [37] Cf. *Jude, 3*? [38] Lit. : was given in affection(s) = *gratiam invenit.* Cf. R. Payne Smith, *Thesaurus syriacus*, col. 1567. [39] *Gen.* 39,4. [40] *Ibid., 21.* [41] *1 Kings* 11,*19*. [42] *Acts* 2,47. [43] *Lk.* 2,52.

to the composition of voice, because *sensation* is one thing and *knowledge which is assembled by doctrine* another. Grace brings (one) to sensation, but knowledge of thoughts is gained from exercise and doctrine, and with them is manifest in the third order faith, which is born of the sound will of the soul. Two are our own, but the other is the gift of God. For that we believe in things which are not understood is of our will, and that we gain knowledge by exercise and by training is of our care, but that we sense spiritual things which (are) inward of word and thought — the grace of God gives (that), sometimes freely, as to the apostles, and sometimes to the purity of the mind, which is gained from victory over the passions. And sensation like this does not come to word nor fall under psychic thoughts, because they too do not become its seers, but to the mind only it is shown by grace and it singly rejoices and takes delight in it. And if * this knowledge is not grasped by thoughts, which are inward of words, how is it to be laid hold of by the composed word and by writings? * p. 67

And if they who sense it are not capable of delivering [it] in word, because sensation, as I have said, does not come to word, how are heretics, who do not even hold the faith about it, to come to the exact interpretation of [it]? For *wisdom dwells not in the soul stained by evil things nor in the body convicted of sin*[44]. But (the heretics) here, who not only are in subjection to passions and exercised in stratagems but are also cut off from the true faith of God, how are they able to understand the wisdom in which Christ grew? And if the wisdom of the apostle, he said, among the perfected is spoken[45] and to them only is revealed, how may this of Christ be known to the heretics, because a simple reading of the Scriptures does not make known the wisdom which is in them, as neither (does) the sight of natures the knowledge hidden in them?

And from the sight of the (created) works everyone who wishes is able to know God, but from the spiritual wisdom in them only they (are able to know him) who have been purified of passions, who have become first finders of their mind and then of that wisdom in which the mind grows. And they see it not through the bodies (in) which it is clothed but in purity of mind, for that is its nature, when it is purified and casts off from it the old man, that nakedly, without the mediation of bodies, it lights upon spiritual things. And if corporeal[46] rational

[44] *Wisdom* 1,4. [45] Cf. *1 Cor.* 2,6. [46] Cf. above, p. 11, n. 9.

(beings) had been able without the sight of bodies[46] to sense the knowledge of God, he would not have created the visible things, but because he willed to make not only rational spiritual (beings) but also man, who is composed from soul and body, for the exercise of (man) he put wisdom in bodies, in order that as he sees, hears, tastes, smells and touches he might gather knowledge to himself—not spiritual, but this (one) which is connected to things. For that one, as I have said, * p. 68 is gained not by exercise but only by purity * of mind, and exercise, reading and inquiry about every thing finds this one, but that one —the grace of God shows it to the mind. This one even he who lives in the old man is able to acquire, but that spiritual one only the new man finds, who is so made known by grace and by works, because when this wisdom was embodied in the (created) works it appeared outside, not because of the spiritual (beings), but that it might gather to it the mind of the corporeal (beings). And although (the mind of the corporeal beings) was not able to see the wisdom from the works, (the wisdom) has not been blotted out but has remained, being clothed by them until the end of the times, and is in the Maker and in the (created) works. And unembodied (beings) are exercised in it even without the mediation of bodies, but men through these, and they who cast off their passions even like the spiritual powers.

But when the time of exercise and of doctrine is ended and that of inheritance and of the kingdom is revealed, wisdom will be gathered into its place and will not be destroyed or perish in the dissolution of compositions. And just as if a man wishes to write in signs a part of the knowledge which is in him and after he has written them effaces them, he destroys the sight and the composition of the signs and not the knowledge which was mixed in them, so also God, who inscribed his wisdom in the signs of bodies, when he will abolish composition, that is change it in the renewal, will not destroy his wisdom in them; but likewise it also will be in him without change and in the renewal of bodies without damage, because when he was mixing it in them it did not depart from him but is believed to be in him and in the (created) works—in him not composed, and with the (created) works in compositions and in bodies.

And because the discernment of men did not consent without the reading of these signs to find their writer and also understand the knowledge in them, God showed it another way by which it might proceed to him and in another order taught it wisdom. And in the place of having incorporated * in the (created) works in the beginning the * p. 69 wisdom of his creation, now, at the end of the times, the wisdom of his nature was embodied and became flesh, for *Christ is the power and the wisdom of God*[47]. And while this wisdom which had been embodied grew in stature, it gathered to it through growth that wisdom which had been mixed in the works, and that which will become in the Father at the end of the times...

FRAGMENT 50. LUKE 3,21 [1]

Thus he prayed: *I indeed, O Father, according to thy will have become man, and from when I was born from the virgin until now I have completed these things of human nature and kept, indeed fulfilled, the commandments, mysteries, and types of the law. And now I have been baptised and have prepared baptism that it may become the spiritual womb which gives birth to men anew. And as John was the last of the legal priests, so I have appeared the first of the evangelical priests. But thou, O Father, through my prayer, open heaven and send thy Holy Spirit upon this new womb of baptism! And as he dwelt in the womb of the virgin and embodied me from her, so may he dwell in this womb of baptism and sanctify it, and form men, and cause them to be born of it new sons, and make them your sons, my brothers and inheritors of the kingdom. And that which the priests of the law from Aaron to John could not effect, may the priests of the new covenant be able to do, these to whom I have become first-fruits and first by this prayer. And whenever they baptise and pray to you and ask, send the Holy Spirit upon the baptism by which they are baptised! While now he, the Spirit, with me is appearing openly, may it be known that with them too he descends, secretly, and fulfils through their hands the service of* * *the new* * p. 70 *covenant, for which I have become man and as high priest I pray before you.*

[47] *1 Cor*. 1,*24*.

Fr. 50 [1] **Introduction**: Of the holy Mar Philoxenus.

FRAGMENT 51. LUKE 3,22

... the resurrection of Christ, that his soul was not left in Sheol, nor did his body see corruption[1]. And also our Lord himself teaches that he had not only the body of men, but also the soul: *On account of this my Father loves me, that I lay down my soul that I may take it again*[2]; and further, *I have power to lay down my soul and I have power to take it again*[3]; and further, *The good shepherd lays down his soul for his flock*[4]. And in another passage it is written that he said, *Behold, now is my soul troubled, and what shall (I) say? "Father, save me from this hour"? But for this I have come to this hour*[5].

And the writings of the evangelists make known what things came from him at the hour of his prayer, that when the time of his passion arrived he was afraid and trembled and was troubled[6] as man and said to his disciples, *My soul is sorrowful unto death*[7], and that *he withdrew from them*[8] and *fell upon his face*[9] *and prayed*[10] to his Father with passion as man filled with grief and sorrow and gripped by the fear of death. And terror prevailed over him to this extent, that he did not eschew openly saying, *My Father, if it is possible, let this cup pass by me*[11], not only one time, but even two and three (times)[12]. And when he had come to know the will of his Father, as he desired this (thing) more than that he should not die he said (it) to him, *May not therefore my will come to be, but thine*[13]. And although indeed he was afraid as man, because the event of death troubled also him as (it does) every man, far dearer (to him was) the will of his Father than (his) love of human life. And further, it is written in that place that *being in dread he prayed earnestly and his sweat became like drops of blood,*
* p. 71 *and he fell * upon the ground*[14]. *And there appeared to him an angel who strengthened him*[15]. And in order that it may be known that Jesus is God become man, more than anyone he was brought down and tempted by human passions[16], for in the case of the rest of men nature itself suffices to assure their corporality, but in the case of Christ, with sight and touch and the genuine nature of the body, (there were) also needs and passions by which he was tempted far more deeply and greatly than anyone. And if not, who is there from among men over

Fr. 51 [1] *Acts* 2,*31*. [2] *Jn.* 10,*17*. [3] *Ibid., 18.* [4] *Ibid., 11.* [5] *Jn.* 12,*27*. [6] Cf. *Mt.* 26,*37*; *Mk.* 14,*33*. [7] *Mt.* 26,*38*; *Mk.* 14,*34*. [8] *Lk.* 22,*41*. [9] *Mt.* 26,*39*. [10] *Ibid.*; *Mk.* 14,*35*; *Lk.* 22,*41*. [11] *Mt.* 26,*39*. [12] Cf. *ibid., 42-44*; *Mk.* 14,*39-41*. [13] *Mk.* 14,*36*; *Lk.* 22,*42*. [14] *Lk.* 22,*44*. [15] *Ibid., 43.* [16] Cf. *Heb.* 2,*18*; 4,*15*.

whom the fear of death ruled to this extent, that *his sweat like drops of blood should fall upon the ground*[17] and he should be so immersed in sleep that he should not be awakened from his sleep by the disturbance of the storms nor the noise and clamour of the sailors and of the disciples nor the tossing of the boat[18]? Therefore that his corporality might not be thought false because of his divinity and (that) his passions might not be considered an illusion and his needs a likeness because of the great things of his essence, more than a natural man he was tempted by human things.

And that this economy (is) wise the opinion of the heretics indeed testifies, for if after all these things they have rejected his corporality, what is the error which they would not have introduced if one of the things which are written had been omitted, even although one of the apostles of our Lord openly said that *every spirit which does not confess that Jesus came in flesh is not of God but of the false Christ*[19]? Thus the spirit of that one speaks through the heretics who deny the corporality of the Word and reject his genuine becoming by which men have become sons of God. Simon Magus, who (was) the first of the apostles of Antichrist, said about Jesus that he is not man in truth but in likeness appeared so. And because Eutychians, Marcionites, Valentinians and Manicheans have his opinion about Christ, the right thing is that they should be reckoned like him — and especially these who are near us and are with us and are considered sons of the common congregation and disciples of the faith.

* How therefore may the corporality of Christ be compared, O heretic, with the likeness of the dove in which the Spirit appeared[20]? All these things, and more than these, the Scriptures teach about his corporality — and he only appeared as (did) the Holy Spirit? And look, the likeness of the dove, as they say, no one saw except John alone[21], but everyone looked upon Jesus and all eyes observed his body, his needs and his passions. And his stature with [its] changes was evident to a great number of Jews, and because of his long growth in their presence and the simpleness of his appearance, he seemed to them the son of Joseph. * p. 72

And furthermore, for if the corporality of God is a likeness, also the benefits which have been prepared by [it][22] for men are likenesses.

[17] *Lk.* 22,*44* (cf. above, n. 14). [18] Cf. *Mt.* 8,*24*; *Mk.* 4,*37-38*; *Lk.* 8,*23-24*.
[19] *1 Jn.* 4,*3*. [20] Cf. *Mt.* 3,*16*; *Mk.* 1,*10*; *Lk.* 3,*22*; *Jn.* 1,*32*. Cf. below, n. 43.
[21] Cf. *Jn.* 1,*32*. [22] Cf. below, n. 30.

For on this account he became man, to make us sons to his Father. He was manifested a corporeal (being) to change us to his spirituality. He was born of woman [23] to give birth to us of the Holy Spirit. He received circumcision and kept the law to free us from its subjection and redeem us from its curse [24]. He grew in stature [25] to bring us to completeness and perfection. He was obedient to the parents by grace [26] to make us neighbours and fellow dwellers to the Father by nature. He was baptised by John as man to fashion for us the other womb which bears sons of God. He fasted and hungered and was tempted to give us victory over all the passions of sin. He conquered the Tempter in the wilderness that we might no longer become his subjects but the masters of his contest. He endured passions [27] and *tasted death* [28] to give by his passions impassibility and to justify by his death eternal life. He became a dweller in earth to make us inhabitants of heaven. He was numbered with men [29] to join us with the spiritual powers. And if the corporality which prepared for us these things is a likeness, so also are all the things which became through it [30] an illusion, the salvation of Christ is a false appearance and the blessings which he promised are as far as word only. And according to the
* p. 73 word of Paul, *empty is the preaching* of the apostles * *and the faith* of Christians [31], for if the cause of the benefits is a likeness, what then are they to be reckoned? Perhaps not even thus, but something lesser and lower than this.

And look, the Spirit appeared not to the eye of the body, but he was manifested in a revelation to the mind, as also the prophets of old were used to seeing: as *I saw the Lord, who was sitting upon a high throne, and the whole host of heaven was standing above him* [32]; and as *In the year that king Uzziah died I saw the Lord, who was sitting upon a high and exalted throne, and his glory was filling his temple, and the Seraphim were standing above him* [33]; and as *I saw, and behold, the Spirit was coming from the north. (There was) a great cloud, and fire was breaking out and flashing round about it* [34]; and as *I saw the Lord, who was standing upon a wall of adamant, and in his hand (was) an adamant* [35]; and as *I saw, and behold, thrones were placed and the Ancient of Days took his seat* [36]. In this manner of revelation the Holy

[23] Cf. *Gal.* 4,*4*. [24] Cf. *ibid.* 3,*13*. [25] Cf. *Lk.* 2,*52*. [26] Cf. *ibid., 51*.
[27] Cf. *Heb.* 12,*2*. [28] *Ibid.* 2,*9*. [29] Cf. *Lk.* 22,*37*? [30] Cf. above, n. 22.
[31] *1 Cor.* 15,*14*. [32] *1 Kings* 22,*19* (cf. *Is.* 6,*1*). [33] *Is.* 6,*1-2*. [34] *Ez.* 1,*4*.
[35] *Amos* 7,*7*. [36] *Dan.* 7,*9*.

Spirit appeared to John in the likeness of a dove. And as he was variously manifested in these likenesses to the prophets, and not in one appearance to all of them, so also to John he appeared in another form. And as there the diverse likenesses were teaching something, even although it was not evident to everyone, likewise also (did) this appearance in which the Spirit was revealed. And the power of the appearances and of the revelations is not diminished by this, that men are not able to know them accurately, but the more through their incomprehensibility does their greatness appear, for it is manifest to everyone that the things which are known and spoken are inferior to those which are not comprehended and not spoken.

Therefore, if in likeness God appeared man and in truth did not become man and remain God, there is nothing which merits wonder and faith in the economy. Christ, *the likeness* and *the equal* of the Father, *was* not *emptied*, as Paul taught[37]. And *the rich (one) was* not *improverished* and we have not *become rich by his poverty*[38]. And *God did* not *send his Son and he became* not *of woman*[39]. And that (word) is not true, that like the sons also he shared flesh and blood[40]. And * we do not know him in unchanging reality if (it is) because he* p. 74
did not become (that) he did not change. And that he was conceived without marriage and born of a virgin is not a marvel if the body which was conceived and born was only a likeness. And that *God thus loved the world, that he gave his only Son for it*[41] does not make known anything which merits praise if what was given to death is a likeness and not the Son who is truly embodied. Neither, furthermore, was death really manifested if a shadow was tried by it and not a genuine body. With that (there is this), that if there is not a body, neither (is there) a soul, and if this does not exist, where is *I lay down my soul for the flock*[42]? With that (there is) another (fact), that if God did not truly become man, the virgin is not the mother of God, for what was born was a shadow and not God embodied. And as you flee from the snare of the doctrine of Nestorius you fall into the very same. For he said that God was not embodied nor born but dwelt in a man who was born, and he was reckoning the birth (as) that of a temple and not of the Word, of a man and not of God. And it appeared to him that he should say this because he first denied the

[37] Cf. *Phil.* 2,*6-7*. [38] Cf. *2 Cor.* 8,*9*. [39] *Gal.* 4,*4*. [40] Cf. *Heb.* 2,*14*. [41] *Jn.* 3,*16*. [42] *Ibid.* 10,*11*.

becoming of God, because to him who is born it applies that he should first become, and unless he becomes, neither is he born. And because Nestorius rejected this, that God became man, he denied with it also that he was born of the virgin, and he reckoned the birth, as I have said, in nature and in truth (as) that of a man, and in name and in metaphor (as) that of God. For indeed you, if you were seers of your doctrine, would agree with him, for you do not first confess that God truly became man, by which also the birth would be assured.

But you have compared the embodying of the Word with the likeness of the dove in which the Spirit appeared, and you have delivered in writing that as the hypostasis of the Spirit appeared in the likeness of a dove, also the Son was manifested in the likeness of a man[43]. * p. 75 And why (then) was necessary * the womb of the virgin, and the growth of nine months, for him who in truth was not embodied? And why did he not seize a likeness from air or from another place, as the angels sometimes appeared and (as) demons also are accustomed to manifest themselves to men? Or (why did he not) like the Spirit commence and conclude swiftly the vision of his revelation, for it is clear that the moment was a short and swift (one) in which the Spirit appeared to John in the likeness of the body of a dove? Indeed I suppose that (it) was swifter even than the twinkling of an eye. And it is not for us to say from where that likeness was, nor is it right that we should think that the hypostasis of the Spirit was changed into the vision of a dove, nor that he took that likeness from air, nor that it was in heaven. And it is not proper that we should reckon from nothing he suddenly was. But we assent only to what is written and we do not penetrate by inquiry inward of the word, lest error instead of knowledge should light upon us, and wandering instead of truth. And if in this likeness appeared also Jesus to men, why not in the same way was also the manner of his revelation, that a man be suddenly revealed and then hid, like the Spirit in the likeness of a dove and like the Father in diverse visions and like angels in the likeness of men? But the virgin was needed for him, that he might descend into [her] and remain in [her] womb nine months.

Furthermore, going before the prophets spoke concerning him, and the Spirit made known about him through heralds, and types of him

[43] Cf. above, n. 20 and Introduction, p. 11*; cf. further, DE HALLEUX, *Philoxène*, pp. 88-90.

were formed, and figures of him were written down in the Old (Testament), and prophets and righteous (men) waited for the appearance of his birth, and the Fathers longed to look upon the mystery which was effected through him: for *Abraham your father desired to see my day and he saw and was glad*[44]; and also *Many prophets and righteous (men) longed that they might see what you see and they did not see, and to hear what you hear and they did not hear*[45]. And not only did those of former times hope for and await the revelation of this mystery, * but also disciples who became obedient to his faith[46] have * p. 76 in diverse ways died and are dying because of him, and through tortures and sufferings they confess him *before rulers and judges*[47] and preach without fear or shame the new thing which is not known to custom, that God by his (own) will became embodied and was born of a virgin. For if, as their word (says), his appearance is a likeness, the prophets (are) *false* and the apostles (are) lying and the confession of those who died for him (is) *empty*. And not only is *the faith* in the mystery *found* an *empty*[48] (one) and of no avail, but also the mystery itself and the things which have been prepared through it. And the word of the apostle is spoken for it against those who deny it, that *perhaps those also who have fallen asleep in Christ have perished*[49].

Why therefore do they marvel as at a new deed that the virgin conceived without marriage and remained a virgin even after she had given birth, if she conceived a likeness and gave birth to a shadow? For if a genuine, material[50], thick and dense body[50] did not go out through the opening of the womb and it remained sealed, the birth does not merit wonder, for the nature of spirit is accustomed to pass even through places which are more restricted than the womb. It is neither hindered by a (material) body[50], nor does an (organic) body[50] restrain its fineness, nor does anything composed stand against it. And not only the holy angels but also the unclean demons are thus. And (so) we do not marvel if we hear that an angel passes through a (material) body or a demon enters while the doors are shut—where how many times do also sun and air, whose fineness is thicker than theirs, pass through? And they are not withheld by (material) bodies, and if (it is) thus with them, why should we marvel that the Word (as) a spiritual (thing) went out from the virgin and the tokens of

[44] *Jn*. 8,*56*. [45] *Mt*. 13,*17*. [46] Cf. *Rom*. 1,*5*. [47] Cf. *Lk*. 12,*11*; *Acts* 7,*27*; *35* (*Ex*. 2,*14*). [48] Cf. *1 Cor*. 15,*14-15*. [49] *Ibid*., *18*. [50] Cf.above, p. 11, n. 9.

virginity of her who gave birth to him remainded intact, for if it is a likeness according to their opinion, he left spiritually and not bodily? And with this (one must) also (suppose that) he was conceived spiritually, and how then did the manifestation of conception appear in the womb of her who was bearing him? And if, being a spirit, he did * p. 77 not grow little by little * and blow up the womb in which he was conceived, then the virgin was from these about whom the prophet said, *[We] conceived and we writhed (in labour) like these who give birth to spirits* [51], and her conceiving is a manifestation of evil things and not of good things. For indeed for this reason the prophet dealt with that manifestation and said, *Like these, for we conceived and gave birth to spirits, the chastening of the Lord happened to us to no advantage* [52], rather than, *For [we] conceived and gave birth to vain thoughts, like them.* And again, if the virgin like them conceived and gave birth to a spirit which is not embodied, even she is to be reckoned with them.

And what should cause John to cry out, marvelling at the very mystery, and to teach, *The Word became flesh and came to dwell in us* [53]? And he did not say *the likeness of flesh*, which if the embodying were according to your understanding, thus it would have been right that he say. With that (there is) another (fact), that he did not write *became like*, but *became*, for this (*became like*) would correspond with *likeness*, and not that *became*, in that becoming points to true nature, but imitation to both (likeness and nature). And John did not say that the Word *became like* flesh, but that he *became* flesh, in order that by this word (*became*), which applies to all bodies, in that they become when they are not, we might understand that truly the Word became flesh. And by both words we may be made sure in the mystery : by that *became*, and by this *flesh* he became.

But if the heretics still persist in their opinion and say that if he became he was changed, it is sufficient for their condemnation that they use a word of a heresy with which they do not agree. For everywhere they announce that they contend against the Nestorians and fight with the error of those (people). And (so) if they employ their words, they are found striving with themselves. But if they say, *We agree with this, that the Word became flesh* [54], let them eschew that (word) *likeness*, and let them not confess the names and deny the * p. 78 realities. And let them not read one thing and expound * another, for

[51] *Is.* 26,*18*. [52] *Ibid.*, *18*; *16*. [53] *Jn.* 1,*14*. [54] *Ibid.*

the expressions which are said about the faith do not admit of exposition. Thus, *God sent his Son and he became of woman*[55] : as it is written it is to be believed and it does not admit of another meaning. *The Word became flesh and came to dwell in us*[56] : its exposition is [its] reading and faith accepts the same. *We were reconciled to God by the death of his Son*[57] : there is no other meaning to that word. *If he did not spare his Son but delivered him up for us all, how will he not give us everything with him?*[58] : we marvel at the grace of the giver and we do not divide his gift; and we boast that the Father delivered up *his Son* for us to death, and we do not introduce another hypostasis into the name. *God so loved the world that he gave his only Son for it*[59] : we are astonished that the Father loved so much, and we do not inquire as to how his immortal Son died. Therefore if you affirm that *the Word became flesh*, you should not understand for *flesh*, *likeness*, nor for *became*, *became like*, like the Nestorians, who expound the becoming (as) an assumption and say that the Word did not become flesh but assumed the man.

And therefore if the becoming is affirmed by you, (you must agree that) he became flesh and not a likeness, and if it is believed by you that the virgin conceived and gave birth, (you must agree that) a body went out from her and not a shadow. And for this reason (the fact) that after she gave birth she remained a virgin is believed (to be) a marvel, for if a likeness, which has no genuine body, went out from her and she remained a virgin after the birth of it, what was done in connection with her was not a new thing, and (the fact) that she conceived is not an amazing (thing) if she conceived a likeness and not a genuine body. It is right that everyone who is conceived and born must be related by nature to her who gives birth to him, and this is common to all the born; that on this account also the Son, when he came to the second birth, first became man and became related to his mother by nature, and then was born of her and was named her son; (and) that if he is not like her, * neither is he her son, * p. 79
or that if he is only believed a likeness, of necessity also she who gave birth to him should be so confessed. But if she is by nature a woman, and concerning this, as I believe, not even with you is there a division, also he who was born of her is like her from every way, and on this account he is son and she is mother. And the things which it would

[55] *Gal.* 4,*4*. [56] *Jn.* 1,*14*. [57] *Rom.* 5,*10*. [58] *Ibid.* 8,*32*. [59] *Jn.* 3,*16*.

be right that they be written by us against the Nestorians, your ignorance compels us to say to you, for while you agree with their doctrine you speak against them. If therefore God did not become man in truth but only assumed the likeness or was embodied in imitation, his "mother" is not the *mother* of God. And furthermore, if he assumed the man who became without marriage and he himself did not in truth become, so also the virgin is not to be known the mother of *God*. And this very thing is said by both heretics about the beginning of the economy. And it is clear that also (the same applies) to the rest (of it), for if the birth is a likeness, also the needs and passions of our Saviour are an imitation and he did not *fast and hunger*[60] in truth, and he did not labour and sit down and slumber and sleep[61] and suffer and die (in truth), as the Scriptures teach, but all of them are connected to the way in which he was born of the virgin. And his circumcision[62] and the growth of his stature[63] and *he was twelve*[64] and *thirty years*[65] are not in truth (if the birth is a likeness).

But if they say, *Look, the apostle said that he took the likeness of a servant*[66], *and also that God sent his Son in the likeness of the flesh of sin for sin*[67], they stumble against their opinion and not against the words of Paul, who in his first word placed two likenesses by the side of one another and at first called Christ *the likeness of God*[68] and then *the likeness of a servant*[68]. And he gave a demonstration concerning each likeness from its associate, in order that he who like
* p. 80 you falsifies his likeness of us * may be proved wrong by that *he is the likeness of God*[68], and he who like the Nestorians is false to this may be confuted by that *the likeness of a servant*[68]. So then Paul in both likenesses...

Fragment 52. Luke 3,23

... which are done upon the book of Matthew, we shall pass on to these of the rest, and we shall understand that in two births Christ has been made known in his economy: one from the virgin and the other from the baptism. And like him (are) also those who become members of him, in that first they are born men from the womb, and

[60] *Mt.* 4,*2*. [61] Cf. *Is.* 5,*27*; *Ps.* 121,*4*. [62] Cf. *Lk.* 2,*21*. [63] Cf. *ibid.*, *52*.
[64] *Ibid.*, *42*. [65] *Lk.* 3,*23*. [66] *Phil.* 2,*7*. [67] *Rom.* 8,*3*. [68] Cf. *Phil.* 2,*6*; *7*.

then sons of God from baptism. And he from the womb of nature being God was born man, and we being by nature men have become by this (womb) of baptism sons of God. And Matthew descended through the narration of the generations to the corporeal birth of the Word, and Luke ascended from this (birth) of baptism through the succession of names to God. And he explained that word of the Father which he called out over his Son[1] by (the fact) that he went by succession and brought him up through the [narration of names] to where he was, because it is written that he *went out from* God *and came into the world*[2] ... [the birth] from baptism (is) the true (one), because the birth-giving womb (is) not corruptible, and they who are born from it do not perish, but remain without end spiritual members in the body which they have joined, for it applies to those who have become spiritual (beings) that they remain without dissolution or change.

And when the evangelist compared the birth by nature with this (one) by grace, he called that first (one) *of supposition*, that is, *he was supposed* to be *son of Joseph*[3]. And the word is appropriate to Jesus because he was not son of Joseph in truth, * and to the men who have (* p. 81) become members of him because their first birth (was) not true, and for this reason this second (one) was needed, which makes them not men *of supposition* but sons [to] God. And with nature also the Scripture teaches that our first birth (is) not true but is [only] of appearance and *of supposition*: thus, *Man is like a vapour and [his] days [pass as a shadow]*[4]...

Fragment 53. Luke 3,23

... we understand with (the fact) that *Jesus was supposed son of Joseph*[1] also this, that his members were supposed sons of Adam, because before baptism in supposition they stand men, and after it, furthermore, in supposition they are reckoned sons of Adam, because they become in truth members of Christ and sons of God. And furthermore, it is to be said that they are supposed sons of Adam according to that which he was before his sin, for he did not remain

Fr. 52 [1] Cf. *Lk.* 3,*22*. [2] *Jn.* 16,*28*. [3] *Lk.* 3,*23*. [4] *Ps.* 144,*4*.
Fr. 53 [1] *Lk.* 3,*23*.

as he was and they who were born from him were not like his first formation.

And whereas formerly the human body lived and was upheld by the service of the visible things, now they are upheld by it and it gives back to them the wage of their labour, for through its renewal from death to life and from corruption to incorruptibility they too are coming to the renewal and to the amazing change. And groans are being changed into joys and corruption into incorruptibility, for *all created things are groaning and are in travail until today*[2], calling *today* this world in which, as long as it stands, *all created things are groaning and are in travail* and a type of whose end is that baptism in which Jesus, when he was baptised, fulfilled the will of his Father
* p. 82 and created anew all things visible and invisible. * This is the mystery which was fulfilled in the baptism of our Saviour, which (baptism) indeed the Father ratified through his voice and the Spirit by his descent. And after (he had related that Jesus) made new his members through his baptism, Luke brought them up through the succession of the names which he related up to Adam, and instead of mortal and corruptible (beings) he showed them on account of him (to be) in another order and so brought them to the Father.

But, furthermore, we may say that *supposed* in the other sense, that whereas the Jews were formerly in supposition reckoned sons of God but (as) men (were) in truth sons by grace, today (the members) in supposition are known men and in truth (are) sons of God, because the adoption which they have received will not be taken away or changed but is their permanency corresponding to the hypostasis in which they have become members. And furthermore, as (it applies) to Christ it will be written by us on the other hand, that because with the Jews he was supposed son of Joseph[3], and also his mother spoke with him according to this supposition[4], and also Luke in this manner had written the things which had been told : as *when his parents brought in the child Jesus*[5], and also *his parents went every year to Jerusalem at the feast of the Passover*[6]—for the remedy of these Luke said here that *he was supposed*[7] ...

[2] *Rom.* 8,*22*. [3] Cf. *Mt.* 13,*55*; *Lk.* 4,*22*; *Jn.* 1,*45*; 6,*42*. [4] Cf. *Lk.* 2,*48*.
[5] *Ibid.*, *27*. [6] *Ibid.*, *41*. [7] *Lk.* 3,*23*.

Fragment 54. Luke 3,23

... through that *let us make man according to our image and according to our likeness*[1]. And because especially in baptism this likeness is revealed in us, from [it] he began the narration of the names, from where we become like God and members of his Son. And (there) has been made known to us ascent and descent in the account of the two evangelists. And with the succession * of the corporeal race of men (* p. 83) Matthew descended to the corporeal birth of the Son of God, and with the growth of their renewal, which becomes from baptism, Luke ascended until he brought them to God. And indeed *the ladder* which Jacob saw is set down before us (as) a type of this descent and ascent, *which stood on the earth, and the head of which reached to heaven, and on which the angels of God were ascending and descending, and above which the Lord was standing*[2]. And while one may equate that revelation with the descent of Jacob to the house of Laban and his [ascent] from there, it fits especially, as I think, these things of ours.

But, furthermore, it is evident that not all of them who now are made worthy of this mystery sense it through baptism, and not all of those into whom at that time it was transmitted and flowed (sensed it through baptism), for at first Seth sensed after the sensation had perished from Adam, and after him Enoch, and after him Noah, and then Shem, and after them Abraham, Isaac and Jacob and the rest who imitated their works and their faith. And today, when it has been given in common to everyone, to the sensation of it come (only) they who through labours and sundering cast off from themselves the old man and live in the way of life of the new man[3]. Yet the benefit which formerly flowed through one race—and not through the whole of it, but only one to one they delivered and transmitted it—through baptism has been given freely to all men.

And they may receive the Holy Spirit and become sons of God because *the Word became flesh*[4]. And he received a soul, and rightly with him so the matter was appointed, because flesh needs a soul and both (need) the Holy Spirit. And as flesh when it receives a soul becomes a man, so a man when he receives the Holy Spirit is known a son to God. And whereas flesh receives a soul within the womb, in

Fr. 54 [1] *Gen.* 1,*26*. [2] *Ibid.* 28,*12-13*. [3] Cf. *Col.* 3,*9-10*. [4] *Jn.* 1,*14*.

* p. 84 baptism * the Holy Spirit is given to man, which first, as the first-fruits, (Christ) received...

Fragment 55. Luke 3,23[1]

Matthew wrote down the natural generations and for this reason said that a certain one begat a certain one, but Luke (wrote down) the legal (generations) and for this reason wrote that *he was supposed*[2].

Fragment 56. Luke 3,23-38

...and of forgiveness, that *not only seven times but seventy times seven times* he should forgive offenders[1], he showed it indeed through his passions, he who perhaps while pointing to this of his reminded Simon about that number which was said by Lamech: *Because Cain has been avenged seven times, but Lamech seventy times seven times*[2].

Cain therefore asked of God that because he had killed he might die, who said to him, *Not so, for whoever would kill Cain would let loose seven penalties*[3]. But this (means), *He who would kill you would do a favour for you, in that you would be delivered from the punishment which I have decreed for you. But this which is (the fate) of all killers, that he who sheds the blood of man by man shall his blood be shed*[4], *will not happen to you, but you who have become the demonstrator of killing will be paid back seven times.* And this word may be understood in these senses: that either Cain received seven punishments because he had killed; or that seven generations he remained alive being * p. 85 tormented; or that he who would kill him would spare * him from seven chastisements; or that in the judgement to come his punishment will be much greater than [that of] all killers; or that after he is punished (there) will be an [end] to his sentence and he will be deemed worthy of mercy. That this perhaps may happen to him (is) because he was not the inventor of killing, but served the will of another, him about whom Christ said, *From the beginning he was a murderer and does not*

Fr. 55 [1] **Introduction** *GB*: But Philoxenus of Mabbug in that head *Jesus was about thirty years old* (*Lk.* 3,*23*) wrote thus; *BS*: But Philoxenus said. [2] *Lk.* 3,*23.*

Fr. 56 [1] Cf. *Mt.* 18,*21-22.* [2] *Gen.* 4,*24.* [3] *Ibid., 15.* [4] *Gen.* 9,*6.*

stand in the truth[5]. And he was pointing either to that (fact) that Satan brought in death through the transgression of the commandment, or to this, that he killed Abel by means of Cain. And whereas there through Eve he brought in death upon Adam, here through Cain he killed Abel. And concerning these things everyone may think as he wishes.

Therefore after Cain had killed, he received these punishments which are written, and *a mark* was also placed on him lest he should be destroyed by anything[6]—not only by a man or by an animal, but also (so that) he should not be burned by fire nor drowned by water, for it is likely that he would have thrown himself either into fire or into water to escape from the torments in which he was. And (so) the mark was placed on him so that not even by these things should he be destroyed, and irrational natures also recognised the mark upon him. For he who desired of God that *anyone who found him might kill him*[7] could not the more destroy himself, and rightly has been called *mark* the invulnerability which was placed on him[6]. For how is it not a miracle that flesh should fall into fire and not be burned and into water and not be drowned and be thrown before animals and not be eaten?

And after these things which were said in connection with him, it is written that *Cain went out from before the face of the Lord and dwelt in the land of Nod, opposite Eden*[8], in order not to remain in the neighbourhood of the garden, as Adam and they who [were] descended from Seth were dwelling in this place. And the land in which the garden was planted was called Eden[9], and that in which Cain dwelt the land of Nod. And about Adam it is said that *God expelled him and made him dwell opposite the garden of delights*[10], and about * Cain that *he dwelt in the land of Nod, opposite Eden*[11], that it may be known from these that Adam was dwelling outside the garden in the land of Eden and Cain outside of it (—the land of Eden—) in that which was called the land of Nod. * p. 86

And after Cain had lived in this land, a son was born to him, and he, who afterwards first *built a city*, called him Enoch, and Cain (then) *called the city by the name of his son*[12]. And while it seems that Adam and these who (were descended) from him were dwelling in tents,

[5] *Jn.* 8,*44*. [6] Cf. *Gen.* 4,*15*. [7] Cf. *ibid.*, *14*; *15*. [8] *Ibid.*, *16*. [9] Cf. *Gen.* 2,*8*. [10] *Ibid.* 3,*24* (*25* LXX). [11] Cf. above, n. 8. [12] *Gen.* 4,*17*.

they who were descended from Cain built for themselves a city ... [fear] of animals and of injury ... because they had been cast off from the care of God or because they loved the earth and living in it more than these of the house of Seth, where we see that indeed all the construction and beauty [of cities], walls and decorated habitations were invented by them who particularly have [worldly] thoughts, by these about whom the prophet said: *On ashes their heart [feeds and causes (them) to go astray]; they go astray*[13]. For behold, the patriarchs of the house of Abraham and Isaac and Jacob dwelt in tents, as the apostle said[14], *who were awaiting the city which has [a foundation], whose [builder and maker] is God*[15]. And Adam and the race of Seth perhaps in this sense did not build for themselves a city as (did) the house of Cain, for they indeed were [made heirs] to the habitation of the garden from [which] they had gone out, rather than that land in which they were settling. But the Scripture finds fault with Hezekiah because he built and fortified the walls of Jerusalem and newly brought water into it[16]. And (as regards the fact) that it is written about David that he built the stronghold of Zion and called it by his name[17], it is likely that he did not do this in human thought, but because Solomon built the temple, he previously built the city in [which] the temple would be placed and in which would be established that kingdom which was given to him in type (of that to come). And if he had been forgiven by God, he would have built the temple also. And the city ...

p. 87

Fragment 57. Luke 3,23-38

... the generations which are written, and from it it was embodied and was born bodily, and from baptism it was announced and made known openly through the testimony of the Father and of the Spirit. And Luke, making known who is he who was revealed through the testimony, adds to *this is my beloved Son in whom I am well pleased*[1] that *Jesus was about thirty years old*[2]. And he went by succession and brought him up through the narration of the names up to God the Father, who in the beginning placed the figure in the formation of

[13] *Is.* 44,*20*. [14] Cf. *Heb.* 11,9. [15] *Ibid.*, *10*. [16] Cf. *2 Chron.* 32,*4-5*; *Is.* 22,*9-11*. [17] Cf. *2 Sam.* 5,*9*.

Fr. 57 [1] *Mt.* 3,*17*; (*Mk.* 1,*11*; *Lk.* 3,*22*). [2] *Lk.* 3,*23*.

Adam and descended (and) testified about it in the Jordan, *This is my beloved Son* [3].

For Adam, when first he was created by God, received two things: that he should become the likeness, and should transmit the likeness. And after he sinned, both of them were taken away from him. And that he was not the [image] of God [after] his sin (the fact) that he sensed his nakedness testifies [4], for it is clear that there is not in the image of God that which merits shame. And with this (there is the fact) that *he hid among the trees* [5], for the likeness does not hide from its archetype. And also (the fact) that as a fearful and deceitful (man) he answered when questioned, for none of these things fits with the image of God. And through these Adam has been shown not to have been the likeness of God after his sin — and also from the punishment which he received, and from (the fact) that he became a mortal (being), and from (the fact) that the earth was cursed in his labour [6], and from (the fact) that in pains he gathered food [7], and from (the fact) that (God) decreed for him, *Dust you are and to dust you shall return* [8], and from (the fact) that he said about him when deriding him, *Behold, Adam has become as one of us* [9], and from *lest he take from the tree of life and eat and live forever* [10]. From these and such like we learn that the likeness of God was effaced from Adam after his sin. And that was taken from him (in respect of) that likeness the other thing (which he had received), that it was proceeding through his race, (that) was shown by (the fact) that it was not transmitted into Cain when he was born, nor into Abel * who (was born) after him. And that by the offering of Abel and his murder, which is a figure, it [was restored] to him, (the fact) that it was found with Seth and he gave it to Enosh and *from then he trusted to call on the name of the Lord* [11] testifies. And with these (that is also made clear) because the Scripture narrated here words which are like those which were said at the creation of Adam — *This is the book of the generation of men*, and further, *On the day that God made Adam, for the image of God he made him, male and female he made them* [12] — in that because to Seth and to Enosh was restored the honour which had been taken away from Adam, the words which are written about that one's honour were said.

* p. 88

[3] Cf. above, n. 1. [4] Cf. *Gen.* 3,*7*. [5] *Ibid.*, *8*. [6] *Ibid.*, *17* (*18* LXX). [7] Cf. *ibid.* [8] *Gen.* 3,*19*. [9] *Ibid.*, *22*. [10] *Ibid.* [11] *Gen.* 4,*26*. [12] *Ibid.* 5,*1-2*. Cf. below, n. 14.

And that Adam became the likeness of God is made known through (the fact) that it is written that *God said, "Let us make man according to our image and according to our likeness; and let them rule over the fishes of the sea and over the* [*birds*] *of the heaven*"[13]. And that the image of God became in him we understand from that *God created Adam for his image, for the image of God he made him, male and female he made them*[14]—in that because the sons who transmit this likeness become from the association of both, it said *male and female he made them*. And in order to teach us this understanding, it made its word double and added [to] *God said, "Let us make man according to our image and according to our likeness"*, also that *God created Adam for his image*. And it showed that not only did he become the likeness of God, but also God was placed in him to proceed through his generations. All the more (this fact), that it is not the custom for Scripture to repeat a word which makes known (only) one understanding but here (it did repeat a word), has clearly taught both of them, that he became in the likeness of God, and (that) he received the image of God to be transmitted through his seed. And through that first, [*God*] *said*, "[*Let us make*] *man according to our image and* [*according to our likeness*"], we recognise the hypostasis of the Father, but in that second, *God made man, for the image of God he made him*, we perceive the Son of God, because not only the Father is God by nature, but also the Son. And the Father as the archetype said that man should become, and the Son as the fulfiller of his Father's will made man.

* p. 89 * And that at the creation of man the blessed Moses wrote this word twice did not suffice, but also at the birth of Seth and of Enosh he recalled it and said, *This is the book of the generation of men. On the day that God made man, for the likeness of God he made him*[15]. That is, when the Son made Adam, for the likeness of God the Father he made him. And he narrated [again] the word also with Seth, not in order to show by it that Adam had become (again) in the likeness of God, but that the likeness of God had become (again) in him. That is, that the Son came to lodge in his first formation in order to be transmitted through his generations. And that he said, *Male and female he made them*[16], (is) because from the association of man and of woman is born he who becomes the transmitter of the likeness, and

[13] *Ibid.*, 1,*26*. [14] *Ibid.*, *27*. Philoxenus seems here to have read ܟ as *pro*.
[15] *Gen.* 5,*1*. [16] *Ibid.* 1,*27*; 5,*2*.

for this reason where it is written that man [became] in the likeness of God, it was not [necessary] that *male and female he made them* should be put down, but only *Let us make man according to our image and according to our likeness*. And after Adam had become in the likeness of [God] and [it had been taken away] from him, also (that happened to) Eve, and [as he is] her cause [in] construction [17], also he is (her cause) in honour.

But there are some who say that *God said, "Let us make man according to our image and according to our likeness"* [18] is the plan and the deliberation, and that which is written afterwards, *God made man in his image* [19], (is) the fulfilment of the plan. But it is not likely to be so, because God everywhere with the word manifests the work and does not need to think and deliberate and (only) then make. As *God said, "Let light become"*, and with the word it is written that *light became* [20]. And the work did not lag behind the command, even a little moment, nor was it necessary that he should say forth the word and then should appear that which becomes, but [immediately] that he spoke, the light became from nothing without delay. And that which is written before it, *In the beginning God created heaven and earth* [21], is also to be [reckoned] like it, that at the moment that he willed to create these primary natures, at the moment of his will, the works appeared. And although * he possesses without beginning the will * p. 90
by which he created the created things, it, the creation, was made in the beginning. And immediately that he willed that it should become, suddenly [at once] it was, as he had willed to make it. And not after his word (of command) came (that first word of Scripture), for perhaps it—the word (of Scripture)—was the work in order that by [it] may be figured that form of word coming at the end, *Let man become*. And after God had created heaven and earth by his will and had made the light by his command, it is further written that *God said, "Let a firmament become in the midst of the waters, and let it separate between waters and waters"* [22]. And it became at once as he spoke, and the work did not lag behind the word. And again after these he said, *Let the waters be gathered together* [23], and *Let the earth* [*put forth*] *animal life* [24], and *Let lights become in the firmament of heaven* [25], and *Let the waters breed reptiles* [26], and *Let the earth put forth* [27]. And

[17] Cf. *ibid.* 2,*21-23*. [18] *Ibid.* 1,*26*. [19] *Ibid., 27*. Cf. above, n. 14. [20] *Ibid., 3*. [21] *Ibid., 1*. [22] *Ibid., 6*. [23] *Ibid., 9*. [24] *Ibid., 24*. [25] *Ibid., 14*. [26] *Ibid., 20*. [27] *Ibid., 11; 24*.

everywhere the work adhered to the word, for the command of God has this power, as *he calls they that are not as they are*[28]. For like them is also *Let us make man according to our image and according to our likeness*[29], in that at the moment of the word man became. And even if the manner of his becoming [differs] from the rest of the [works], and if to another he said, *Let us make*, so neither was the work lagging behind the word. As the light was not set back from the word which said, *Let it become*, nor the firmament from the command which stretched it out, so neither (was) the construction of man from that cry which said, *Let us make* [*man*]. And if to the Son the Father gave the command, *Let us make*, so also without delay did the work appear, and the hypostasis of the Son was revealed through (the fact) that the Father [said] to him, *Let us make*.

But if from (the fact) that the word was [repeated] it seems to some that man was not made [immediately], but the thought and the deliberation [preceded] and then the work appeared, not once would Adam be found to have become, but twice: first through *God made man in his image*[30], and secondly through *God formed man (of) the dust from the ground and breathed into his nostrils the breath of life*[31]. * p. 91 Because * they say that that first (one) was the plan and preparation, that is that God first thought and then made man, (it would be) as if these primary things had been created without [thought]. But it is not so, but (as to the fact) that in that *Let light become*[32] it was created immediately, and in that *Let a firmament become in the midst of the waters*[33] it was made without delay, so also in this *Let us make man according to our image and according to our likeness*[34] it is clear that suddenly and without delay man was formed [in the likeness] and in the image of God. And in that which (comes) after it, *God made man for his image, for the image of God he made him*[35], (it is clear) that the likeness of God was placed in him, that is the Son of God dwelt in the formation of man in order to proceed and be transmitted through his generations. But (as for) that third (one), *God formed man (of) the dust from the ground and breathed into him the breath of life*[36], by it Moses showed from what the body was created and from where the life was breathed. As he did also with the construction of woman, that after he had written that *male and female he created them*[37], he

[28] *Rom.* 4,*17*. [29] *Gen.* 1,*26*. [30] *Ibid.*, *27*. [31] *Gen.* 2,*7*. [32] *Ibid.* 1,*3*. [33] *Ibid.*, *6*. [34] *Ibid.*, *26*. [35] *Ibid.*, *27*. [36] *Gen.* 2,*7*. [37] *Ibid.* 1,*27*.

taught how Eve was made and said : *The Lord God caused a stupor to fall upon Adam, and he slept, and he took one of his ribs and filled up the flesh* [*in its place*]*; and the Lord God built the rib which he had taken from Adam into a woman*[38]. And through these he made known from where Eve was made and in what manner, and not twice did he write about her creation.

But if because the word was repeated they go astray and suppose that not where *God said*, "*Let us make man*"[39] did he create Adam, but there he thought and planned and afterwards he made him, also with the creation of these other things it is necessary for them so to suppose. [For] it is written concerning the becoming of the [animals] and of the firmament that *God said*, "*Let the earth put forth animal life according to its kind : cattle and animals and reptiles of the earth according to its kind*"[40], and after this that [*God made the animals*] *of the earth according to* [*their*] *kinds and the cattle according to* [*their kinds*] *and all the reptiles of the earth according to their kinds*[41]. And while it is clear that * they were created by the first command, the * p. 92
word was repeated to [teach that] that which God commanded became. And [furthermore], also concerning the lights it is written that [*God*] *said*, "*Let lights become in the firmament of heaven to give light upon the earth*"[42], and shortly after it repeats the word and says, *It became so, and God made the two great lights*[43]. And this type of word we find with all the works, that although by the first command they were made, it may make double the word concerning them and make known that that which God said became. And comparing with these also the creation of man, we learn that in that *God said*, "*Let us make man according to our image and according to our likeness*"[44], he too was created. And (so) if words are written which are like this (first one), they make known something other which we showed in our previous words.

Therefore the faithful image of the Father, the Son by nature, was placed in the likeness which became for him, and proceeded and was transmitted through all the [generations] as far as the [virgin]. And because of him were [preserved] ... the care of his Father ... Isaiah [the prophet : *As is found*] *the grape-seed in* [*the cluster*] ... ["*Do not*] *destroy it, because* [*there is a blessing*] *in it*", *so* [*I will do because of*] ... *and because of this* [*I will not destroy them all. And I will bring forth*] *seed*

[38] *Ibid.* 2,*21-22*. [39] *Ibid.* 1,*26*. [40] *Ibid.*, *24*. [41] *Ibid.*, *25*. [42] *Ibid.*, *14* (cf. *15*). [43] *Ibid.*, *15-16*. [44] *Ibid.*, *26*.

from Jacob [*and from Judah, and it will inherit*] *my holy mountain*[45]. [And the cluster from] the sword was preserved and not [cut down], according to the word of the prophet, because of the carried grape-seed which was dependent on it. And because the cluster went out from the vine and the grape-seed was dependent on the cluster, we understand the vine (to refer) to the patriarchs of the race, the cluster to their people and the grape-seed to Christ, who was transmitted through their [generations]—he who was planted in Adam through his formation and sprouted from the virgin in *the fullness of the times*[46]. And all the generations in the interval transmitted him, and just as he was * p. 93 transmitted from Adam to the virgin, * also he came from her to baptism, which when he was baptised in it he made the new womb which gives birth to sons of God. And as he who at that very time [fulfilled] the mystery in deed and gained members ... from the womb ... through the succession of the names ... which Luke wrote ... and the children which [God has given][47] ... [without beginning or change, that this] had been known with God the Father without beginning Paul teaches: thus, [*Those*] *whom he fore-knew he also fore-ordained to become like the image of his Son*[48], calling *image* the hypostasis of the Son. For he is truly the faithful image of God the Father, and like [him (are) all] who have become to [him] members by baptism. And because they have been made worthy of such an adoption, he has been called to them, he indeed, the beginning and the first-born : thus, *He is the beginning and the first-born from the dead*[49]; and further, *He might become the first-born of many brothers*[50].

Therefore it has been made known from these things which have been said that not only did the first man become in the likeness of God, but also (he became) the receiver and transmitter of the likeness, that is of the hypostasis of the Son, who is the faithful and natural image of God the Father, concerning whom Lamech prophesied that after [seventy-seven] generations[51] ... and cancel ... the sin of the killing by Cain which ... not make atonement ... these generations ... say.[52]

[45] *Is.* 65,*8-9*. [46] Cf. *Gal.* 4,*4*; *Eph.* 1,*10*. [47] *Is.* 8,*18*; *Heb.* 2,*13*? [48] *Rom.* 8,*29*. [49] *Col.* 1,*18*. [50] *Rom.* 8,*29*. [51] Cf. *Gen.* 4,*24*. [52] **Colophon** A : There is in this book the commentary of five chapters taken from the evangelist Luke.

The end of the fourth book of the commentary of the evangelists Matthew and Luke done by God-loving Philoxenus, bishop of Mabbug. It was copied in the city of Mabbug in the year 822 of Alexander the Macedonian.

Everyone who loves to read should take care also to understand and apprehend, lest he be found to labour in vain.

Glory to Christ Jesus, God [the Word] who was made man. Amen.

INDEX

I. BIBLICAL CITATIONS AND ALLUSIONS

II. NAMES OF PERSONS AND PLACES

CONTENTS

Imprimerie Orientaliste, s.p.r.l., Louvain (Belgique)